FIRST STEPS OF FAITH

EXPLORING YOUR NEW LIFE IN CHRIST

STEVE SHANK

GENERAL EDITOR: C.J. MAHANEY

EXECUTIVE EDITOR: GREG SOMERVILLE

PURSUIT OF GODLINESS
SERIES
PDI
COMMUNICATIONS

PDI Communications is a division of PDI Ministries, which serves a growing network of local churches in the United States and abroad. For information about the ministry or for permission to reproduce portions of this book, please contact us.

PDI Communications
7881 Beechcraft Avenue, Suite B
Gaithersburg, MD 20879

1-800-736-2202
fax: 301-948-7833
email: pdi@pdinet.org
Web site: www.pdinet.org

FIRST STEPS OF FAITH
© 1995 PDI Communications
All rights reserved.

Author: Steve Shank
Cover design: Gallison Design
Book layout: Martin Stanley

Unless otherwise noted, Scripture quotations are taken from *The Holy Bible*, New International Version.
Copyright © 1973, 1978, 1984 by International Bible Society.
Used by permission of Zondervan Bible Publishers.
All rights reserved.

ISBN 1-881039-05-6

Printed in the United States of America

1097

Dedicated to Travis, Jordan, Janelle, and Connor

I hope this book will help you enjoy God and all he has done for you,
because nothing could inspire you more to become what he wants you to be.
Thanks for the fun and laughter you bring to our home,
and for approaching your first steps of faith with diligence.
—Dad

CONTENTS

HOW TO USE THIS BOOK

First Steps Of Faith is one of a series of books published by PDI Communications to equip and motivate Christians. The series is the logical outgrowth of four deeply held convictions:

■ The Bible is our infallible standard for faith, doctrine, and practice. Those who resist its authority will be blown off course by their own feelings and cultural trends.

■ Knowledge without application is lifeless. In order to be transformed, we must apply and practice the truth of God's Word in daily life.

■ Application of these principles is impossible apart from the Holy Spirit. While we must participate in change, he is the source of our power.

■ The church is God's intended context for change. God never intended for us to live isolated from or independent of other Christians. Through committed participation in the local church, we find instruction, encouragement, correction, and opportunities to press on toward maturity in Christ.

With the possible exception of the "Group Discussion" questions, the format of this book is equally suited for individuals and small groups. A variety of different elements have been included to make each study as interesting and helpful as possible.

Bible Study: Begin by digging into God's Word. Unless otherwise noted, all Scripture quotations come from the New International Version (NIV) of the Bible.

Warm-Up: A little mental exercise to get you in the mood.

Personal Study: Here is the meat of the lesson, spiced with occasional questions to help you apply what you're reading.

Margin Questions: If you have the time, dig deeper into the lesson as you *Meditate On...* biblical truths or turn to related passages *For Further Study*.

Group Discussion: Though you may not get past the first question or two, these are guaranteed to get your group thinking and talking about real-life issues.

Recommended Reading: For those who can't get enough of a particular topic, here's a whole bookshelf full of great resources.

While you are encouraged to experiment in your use of this book, group discussion will be better served when members work through the material in advance. And remember that you're not going through this book alone. The Holy Spirit is your tutor. With his help, these studies have the potential to change your life. ■

FOREWORD

We have a deck off our family room. I grill on the deck, my wife has teas on the deck, our four children climb on the deck, our dog scratches on the deck, squirrels drop acorns on the deck, and birds occasionally do things on the deck. Generally speaking, our deck receives constant use and abuse.

During the summer, half of it is sun-scorched while the other half grows fuzzy green stuff beneath the shady canopy of 40-foot oak trees. I have walked barefoot on our deck in the heat of summer when the boards were so hot, they burned my feet. I have looked out our family room windows to see the deck flooded by prolonged rains. I've seen it covered with sleet, frost, and snow, as well as leaves and broken tree limbs.

The fact is, without help, our deck would be a disaster. The boards would warp and splinter. It would eventually sag and rot. The only way our deck can survive its exposure to the elements is if we treat it with a professional grade wood preservative. No superficial gloss-over with cheap materials will do the job. In order to stand up over time, our deck needs a preservative that will be absorbed deep into its fibers and become part of the wood itself. It needs a penetrating preservative that will act as a shield against water and insect damage. It needs a preservative that will help it withstand the heat and the sleet. Unless we are faithful to preserve our deck, we're going to wake up one morning and find it reduced to a pile of firewood.

You may be wondering how a lecture on deck preservation ties in to this book and to exploring your new life in Christ. Actually, there are a lot of parallels.

No life compares to the Christian life. In Christ you have found your heart's desire, your reason for existence. You have begun tasting the many benefits of citizenship in God's kingdom: love, joy, peace, security, hope, and an exciting new purpose for living, to name just a few. And the best is yet to come. However, Scripture tells us that the Christian life is also a challenging life. Though more satisfying than anything else in the world, it requires deep sacrifice. "If anyone would come after me," Jesus said, "he must deny himself and take up his cross and follow me" (Mark 8:34).

As much as we might wish for a cozy, storm-free environment, God rarely provides this for us. Instead, he allows us—and expects us—to grow strong during the heat waves and driving storms of life. Like my deck, Christians cannot successfully weather difficult circumstances with just a superficial preparation. An occasional Bible-reading or sporadic, half-hearted prayer simply won't suffice. Instead, we need something that penetrates. We need truth that becomes part of us, truth that will sustain us through whatever weather might loom on the horizon.

Every Christian will eventually face seasons of heat and drought when God seems distant or uninvolved. There will be times of winter and cold. There will be times when we're deluged by unexpected adversity, trial, and temptation.

I've written this book to help you understand and apply foundational truths from Scripture that will help you through such seasons. By God's grace, it can be a significant source of encouragement, hope, and strength. But just as my deck must absorb preservative to withstand the weather, you will only benefit from *First Steps Of Faith* if its biblical truths sink in deep. Skimming is fine for the sports page, but fatal when pursuing a relationship with God.

Therefore, resist the temptation to breeze through this book; no one is timing you. Each study addresses a topic that is critical to the development of a secure, strong, and successful Christian life. The brevity with which the topics are discussed is no reflection on their importance. Instead, my hope is that you will be inspired to continue on in a lifelong spiritual journey of studying and living God's Word.

God has begun a wonderful work in you. Not only will *First Steps Of Faith* help you enjoy the full benefit of God's work, but I trust it can help you develop a solid faith that won't warp, splinter, or fall apart during the difficult seasons of life. So grab your Bible, a pen, and find a comfortable chair. Let's begin soaking up foundational truths that will become part of us and sustain us for the rest of our lives.

—Steve Shank

Acknowledgments

Greg Somerville—Thanks for your advice and encouragement along the way. Your faith for the project and your expertise were so needed. Enjoy the Red Lobster—you've earned it!

Brent Detwiler—Knowing that you were taking the time to review this manuscript as it took shape was very reassuring to me. I'm inspired by your love for the truth.

My Southside Church family—I don't know what else to say but thanks for all of your prayers and encouragement. I especially want to thank the Southside staff for all the extra work you absorbed so I could finish this project. Pizza is on me. John and Dave, thanks for helping me laugh through the process, even though I know you were laughing at me!

And most of all, Janis—What can I say? With you I'm spoiled rotten. I don't know anyone who sacrifices for others more than you do. Your giving nature and servant's heart make my life the greatest adventure. I couldn't have given this project the attention it needed if it weren't for your being the greatest helpmate of all. IAOAMTMPBOY. (You know what it means…I feel it even more now than the day I had it engraved on your wedding ring. Let's keep the readers guessing!)

WHO MAKES THE FIRST MOVE?

BIBLE STUDY Ephesians 2:1-10

WARM-UP Can you identify any of these "Famous Firsts"?

First head of the U.S. Post Office: _____

First novel written on a typewriter:_____

First state to allow women to vote: _____

First chain store in the U.S.: _____

(See page 14 for answers)

PERSONAL STUDY My family and I live twenty minutes from the ocean. Several times each year we'll gather up our sand pails, plastic shovels, boogie boards, sunscreen, towels, chips, sodas, and six pairs of flip-flops and head off to play in the sand and surf.

The younger children love playing in the waves with me. With Daddy, big and brave, they can venture out farther than they ever would alone. (Little do they know that Daddy, big and brave, is really Daddy, chicken and paranoid, when it comes to young children and the ocean.)

One day my daughter Janelle and I edged out to meet the incessant, rolling swells. Having done this with her many times before, I wasn't surprised when she began her ritual, high-pitched squeal/scream combo—right in my ear. "No, Daddy, let's go back. Daddy, we're toooo faarrr!!! Oh, here comes a wave. Daddy, it's too big. I'm scared!!! No!! NO!! EEEEEKK!!! ... Wow, Daddy, that was neat! Let's do it again!" And we did, over and over and over, with Janelle shrieking hysterically each time (and loving it).

After a few minutes, however, I noticed another routine in my daughter's behavior. Just before getting slammed by a wave, Janelle, who at the time was seven years old and

1

40 skinny pounds, would pull her wrist from my grasp and insist she hang on to me. Each time I got a fresh grip, she pulled away in order to grip *me*. It quickly became obvious that she had more faith in her ability to hang onto me than in my ability to hang onto her.

Now I happen to be six and a half feet tall. My long, bony fingers can almost encircle Janelle's waist, let alone her wrist. But in the face of danger, my little girl felt more secure holding onto my slippery, lotion-smeared fingers than she felt when being held by her Daddy. As I thought about this, the Lord gave me an insight. "Son, many of my children relate to me the same way. They trust in their ability to hang onto me rather than trusting that I am holding onto them."

Meditate on John 10:27-29. Is there anything to fear when Jesus has you in his grip?

Splashing in the waves with Janelle illustrated a critical truth for me. As fallen creatures, we tend to think we're responsible for hanging onto our Heavenly Father. If we have successfully fought the waves of temptation and trial, we feel at peace with God. Our relationship with him seems secure. But when we fall short of God's standards, we can feel distant or even cut off from him. The question boils down to this: *Who is hanging on to whom?* Are we hanging on to a reluctant God who will turn in disgust the moment we mess up? Or is he hanging on to us?

The night I submitted my life to Christ, I assumed I was the one who had made the first move. I thought I had reached out and grabbed God's hand. Like many new Christians, I thought I had "found the Lord." I didn't even consider the fact that perhaps God had reached out and found me.

> **❝** You are loved and accepted by God through the merit of Jesus, and you are blessed by God through the merit of Jesus. Nothing you ever do will cause Him to love you any more or any less. He loves you strictly by His grace given to you through Jesus.[1] **❞**
>
> **—Jerry Bridges**

And yet a careful study of the Bible reveals that *God makes the first move* in bringing people to himself. He sent his son Jesus to die on the Cross for your sin. It is his gracious activity on your behalf that led you to the point of salvation, and it is his hand that holds you securely now. Though you responded to his initiative, even that response was made possible by what he had already done in your life. God deserves all the credit.

Who is hanging onto whom? Answering that question is of foundational importance for your new life in Christ. It could make all the difference between whether you are secure in God's love or striving for his acceptance. That's why these first few pages of this book will explore the events underlying your conversion—the "Eight C's of Salvation." By the time we've finished, I hope you are encouraged to rest in the loving grip of God.

---

1 Which of these would be hardest to hang onto?

❏ A greased pig

❏ A kite in a hurricane

❏ A hyperactive toddler at Disney World

❏ An eel dipped in Vaseline

❏ A $100 bill in a Las Vegas casino

#1: Chosen by God

The first step of your salvation occurred ages before you were born:

> For he chose us in him *before the creation of the world* to be holy and blameless in his sight. In love he predestined us to be adopted as his sons through Jesus Christ in accordance with his pleasure and will. (Ephesians 1:4-5)

Think about that for a minute. Long before you were conceived, God looked down the corridors of time and saw your life. He set his affection on you before you took your first breath. "All the days ordained for me were written in your book *before one of them came to be*," wrote David (Psalm 139:16). Before your grandparents were born— before Adam and Eve themselves were created—God saw the day you would exist and chose you to be his child.

Why did God choose you? It wasn't because you showed potential. It wasn't because your parents presented you to God at the altar while you were an infant. It wasn't because you frantically cried out for help from under the garbage of your sinful life, nor was it a reward for any-thing you had done. In fact, as we've just seen, God chose you before you or anyone else influenced his decision in any way. Scripture says God "saved us and called us to a holy life—*not because of anything we have done* but

For Further Study: Read Job 14:5. From beginning to end, your life has been ordained by God.

because of his own purpose and grace. This grace was given us in Christ Jesus *before the beginning of time...*" (2 Timothy 1:8-9, emphasis added).

It would be nice to think our own wisdom or insight caused us to follow Christ, but it just isn't true. "As it is written, 'There is no one righteous, not even one; there is no one who understands, no one who seeks God'" (Romans 3:10-11). Human hearts don't naturally seek God or submit to him. Quite the opposite. So even though it may be a little hard to swallow, please understand: your longing to know God and be reconciled to him didn't originate in your own heart. It originated with God. It is wonderful evidence that he had chosen you and pursued you, long before you even thought of searching for him.

> ❝ We who are Christ's people were chosen by the Father before the world was created and before any of us existed. The very thought boggles the mind! We shall never be able to understand it; we can only bow our heads in wonder.[2] ❞
>
> **—Anthony Hoekema**

In his infinite mercy, God chose you for himself and set in motion the events leading to your conversion. As Jesus said, "You did not choose me, but I chose you" (John 15:16). Allow your mind to bask in the truth that before time began, the Sovereign God of the universe graciously hand-picked you to be one of his children.

#2: Created by God

God is the author of life. Over and over the Bible tells us each life comes from him. "Your hands shaped me and made me," said Job, a prominent character in the Old Testament (Job 10:8). "All things were created by him and for him," wrote the apostle Paul (Colossians 1:16). Probably the most well-known and intimate account of God's role in creating life was penned by King David in Psalm 139:

Meditate on Matthew 10:30. Though you are just one among billions of people on Earth, God knows every hair on your head!

For you created my inmost being; you knit me together in my mother's womb. I praise you because I am fearfully and wonderfully made; your works are wonderful, I know that full well. My frame was not hidden from you when I was made in the secret place. When I was woven together in the depths of the earth, your eyes saw my unformed body. (Psalm 139:13-16)

4

God decided which cell from your mother's body and which cell from your father's body would unite their unique genetic codes to create the one and only you. Had two other cells been involved, you wouldn't have turned out as you did. You would look like someone else, think like someone else, feel like someone else, be someone else. You are you for one reason only: God wanted to make you this way.

No life is a mistake, even if the circumstances surrounding its beginning seem disastrous. I once heard about a young woman who crumpled in the aisle of her church, sobbing uncontrollably. Years of doubt, years of guilt couldn't pour out of her eyes fast enough. You see, she had spun her self-image around a horrible fact: her mother had been brutally raped. And though urged to have an abortion, her mother had made the difficult decision that the child inside her would live. Now that child needed to know she wasn't a mistake. She needed to be assured there was a reason and plan for her existence.

For Further Study: As you will see in Isaiah 44:2, God's creation of you and his care for you go hand in hand.

I've heard it said there is no such thing as an illegitimate child, only illegitimate parents. There are aspects of God's plan that remain shrouded in mystery. However, we can cling to the truth that God is completely trustworthy. He reigns in sovereign power. And regardless of the circumstances surrounding your conception, God was in control, creating you for his pleasure. He reaches down into even the most devastating situation and redeems it for his glory and your good.

Knowing God created you should bring tremendous security and peace. However, it also brings humility. Had you merely evolved from an ape or a clump of algae, you would be free to do whatever you want in life. But you are the handiwork of your Creator. To borrow an illustration from the prophet Isaiah, you are a pot in the hands of the Master Potter. He is entitled to shape your life in the way he sees best. And in his mercy, he has fashioned you for a noble purpose (Romans 9:21).

---

2 If you could change one thing about yourself or your past, what would it be? Why?

#3: Our Condition

Most people misunderstand their condition before God. They would admit they are sinful, but only in a relative sense. They think in terms of "big" sins and "little" sins. If all they have done is cheat on their income tax or lie to a supervisor, they consider themselves superior to the person who goes out and commits cold-blooded murder. In other words, they assume God will be satisfied with anyone who is basically a "good person."

Such thinking shows a serious ignorance of God's Word. We are not sinners because we sin; the Bible says *we sin because we are sinners.* Our sin is an inherited condition. The moment Adam and Eve disobeyed God, sin polluted humanity's gene pool. Every child born on this planet, with the exception of Jesus Christ, comes fully equipped with a warped, sinful disposition. It's there from the moment of conception. All of our sinful conduct—lying, hatred, jealousy, anger, pride, lust, selfishness, and murder—stems from this condition theologians call "original sin."

> ❟❟ By nature we are well pleased with ourselves, and mad enough to think that we deserve something good at the hands of God.[3] ❞
>
> —A.W. Pink

Here is a biblical diagnosis of the human condition:

Hopelessly separated from God (Ephesians 2:1-3; Colossians 1:21; Romans 6:23). There is simply no way we could ever make ourselves acceptable to the holy and Almighty God.

Spiritually dead (Romans 5:12; Ephesians 2:1; Colossians 2:13).

Hostile toward God (Romans 5:10; Colossians 1:21). Left to ourselves, all of us shake our stubborn fists at the King, Lord, and Ruler of our lives.

Blinded and enslaved by Satan (2 Corinthians 4:3-4; 2 Timothy 2:24-26).

Powerless to overcome sin (Romans 1:28-32, 5:6; John 8:34).

Unable to understand the things of God (Proverbs 14:12; Isaiah 55:8-9; 1 Corinthians 2:14).

Incapable of living a spiritually fruitful and meaningful life (John 15:4-6).[4]

For Further Study:
What sobering truth would a "good person" find in Mark 10:18?

Pretty bleak, isn't it? The Bible doesn't rank sins the way we do. It doesn't grade on a curve. It lumps tax evaders and serial killers together as sinners. Anyone who considers himself or herself "basically a good person" is terribly deceived. Apart from Christ we're all dead, lost, powerless, ungodly, helpless, blind, and enemies of God.

Scripture's assessment may seem depressing, but it is meant to set you free. Once you see your true condition before God, you'll stop doing what my daughter Janelle did. You'll stop trying to hang onto God, and you'll realize how completely dependent you are on him to hang onto you. Your only hope—and what a solid hope it is!—rests on the fact that God devised a way to deliver you from your lost and sinful condition. Let's look at it together.

#4: Called by God

One day when I was a boy I saw my neighbor's cat get hit by a car. Though I didn't care much for cats (and this one was no exception), I felt a twinge of sadness as it flew into the bushes. So I helped my neighbor look for it. "Here kitty, kitty, kitty," I called. Meanwhile I was thinking, *If this cat comes to me now after all the abuse I've given it, it must really be hurt.*

When we finally found it, the poor cat was as dead as Julius Caesar. No amount of calling could have brought it to life. I could have called "kitty, kitty, kitty" all week without getting any response from that flattened feline.

Before you became a Christian, you were spiritually in the same state as my neighbor's cat: dead as a doornail, incapable of any response. Don't take it personally. The Bible says the same about everyone who has yet to be converted: "As for you, *you were dead* in your transgressions and sins, in which you used to live" (Ephesians 2:1,2). Your spirit wasn't merely comatose or unconscious. It wasn't sickly or sluggish. It was dead. Even though God had chosen you and created you, your sinful condition separated you from him.

Meditate on Ephesians 2:12-13.
Where did you once stand in relation to God? Where do you stand now?

The story would have ended there, were it not for God's mercy. Do you realize what he did? "When you were dead in your sins…God *made you alive* with Christ" (Colossians 2:13). Why? *"Because of his great love* for us…it is by grace you have been saved" (Ephesians 2:4-5). Had you done anything to deserve this? "He saved us, *not because of righteous things we had done*, but because of his mercy" (Titus 3:5).

7

For Further Study: If you want to see a fascinating picture of God's ability to breathe life into something dead, read Ezekiel 37:1-14.

One day, in his own perfect timing, God touched the cold, dead center of your spiritual being and brought it to life. You were born again. (Theologians call this event *regeneration*. It is an important word—you will find it many times in this book.) The new birth is the greatest miracle you will ever experience. While you were still spiritually dead, incapable of responding to God and awaiting judgment for your sin, God called you to himself through the message of the gospel, and that call produced life, faith, and repentance. (Something my "kitty, kitty, kitty" never could have done!) God's life-giving call, which some refer to as his effective or effectual calling, is "that mysterious, divine, and humanly inexplicable act of God through the Holy Spirit, which brings us into living fellowship with Jesus Christ, our Lord."[6]

> **❝** Effective calling is an act of God the Father, speaking through the human proclamation of the gospel, in which he summons people to himself in such a way that they respond in saving faith.[5] **❞**
>
> —**Wayne Grudem**

Dead cats don't come crawling out of the bushes when you call them. But when God's call penetrated the deadness and darkness of your soul, it rang with the life-giving power of regeneration. You have been brought from death to life, not by your own effort, but through a miraculous and merciful work of God.

3 Which of the following best describes how God called you to himself?

☐ Someone shared with you one-on-one about Jesus

☐ You came forward during a church service

☐ God spoke to you through a Bible or some other book

☐ You passed a phone booth and heard the phone ringing

☐ Other _____

#5: Cooperating with God

Of all the billions of babies ever born, not one has been able to take credit for its own conception. Likewise, no Christian can claim responsibility for his or her own regeneration. Only God could have brought your dead spirit to life. But once he did that miraculous work, you then needed to cooperate with him through conversion.

Theologian Wayne Grudem defines conversion as "our willing response to the gospel call, in which we sincerely repent of sins and place our trust in Christ for salvation."[7] A genuine conversion involves two responses: faith and repentance. Let's look at these responses separately.

Faith requires believing what God's Word says about your sin and Jesus' sacrifice. By faith you admit that your condition is hopeless, that you are unable to please God, and that your sin has provoked his holy anger. But faith also enables you to accept Christ's death on the Cross as the full, final, and free payment for your sin. Faith is a fascinating thing. It is both a gift from God (Ephesians 2:8) and an act of your redeemed will. In other words, God gives you faith, but you are responsible for exercising it. When he regenerated you God opened your heart, planting the seed of faith by which you trust in Jesus as God's only hope for sinful humanity.

For Further Study: Both Galatians 2:16 and Hebrews 10:38 show the importance of diligently exercising the faith God has given you.

Faith alone is an insufficient response; repentance is also required for conversion. Repentance simply means change. It begins with a change in your view of God. He is now to be your Lord, the ruler of your life. Repentance also involves a change in your view of sin. Instead of doing whatever makes you feel good, you now pass your actions through the filter of God's Word to see if they measure up with his expectations. Finally, repentance requires a change in your view of yourself. Once you exalted yourself and lived for your own pleasure; now you are laying down your life to please the One who created you, died for you, and calls you to obedience.

> ❝ The New Testament word for repentance means changing one's mind so that one's views, values, goals, and ways are changed and one's whole life is lived differently. The change is radical, both inwardly and outwardly...Repentance means starting to live a new life.[8] ❞
>
> —J.I. Packer

Baptism in water should be one of your first acts of obedience as a new follower of Christ (Matthew 28:19). Being baptized publicly in water is a bold testimony to all who witness it that two changes have occurred in your life: first, that God has mercifully regenerated you, and second, that you have consciously turned away from your former way of life. It is "a symbol of beginning the Christian life," writes Wayne Grudem.[9] Please note, however, that baptism isn't what saves you; you have been saved by the sacrificial work of Jesus. Nor does water baptism remove your sinful nature

For Further Study:
Early Christians placed a high priority on water baptism. For a few examples, see Acts 2:41, 8:36-38, 16:33, and 22:16.

or regenerate your soul. Rather, baptism is a sign of your allegiance to Jesus, a declaration that you have been united with Christ in his death and resurrection. Jesus commanded it, the early church modeled it, and you will benefit immeasurably by it. If you haven't already been baptized in water, ask your pastor how you can experience this powerful event.

Faith in Christ and repentant submission to Christ— these are the only appropriate responses to God's merciful initiative on your behalf. They are not mere flags stuck in the soil of your heart to commemorate a one-time event. Instead, they are the twin pillars supporting your new Christian life. You are to live every day cooperating with God by cultivating habits of faith and ongoing repentance.

#6: In Christ

As if regeneration and conversion didn't adequately express the riches of his grace, God has done something more. See if you can piece it together from this passage:

> Don't you know that all of us who were baptized into Christ Jesus were baptized into his death? We were therefore buried with him through baptism into death in order that, just as Christ was raised from the dead through the glory of the Father, we too may live a new life.
>
> If we have been united with him like this in his death, we will certainly also be united with him in his resurrection. For we know that our old self was crucified with him so that the body of sin might be done away with, that we should no longer be slaves to sin—because anyone who has died has been freed from sin. (Romans 6:3-7)

Meditate on Colossians 2:9-10.
Are there any areas of your life where you feel incomplete or insufficient? Let these two verses adjust your perspective!

God has chosen you, created you, called you out of your sinful condition, and enabled you to cooperate with his work through repentance and faith. In addition, he has united you with his Son, Jesus Christ. You are now able to say, like the apostle Paul,

> I have been crucified with Christ and *I no longer live, but Christ lives in me.* The life I live in the body, I live by faith in the Son of God, who loved me and gave himself for me. (Galatians 2:20)

Jesus Christ—the One who triumphed over sin and death—now lives in you. And as Romans 6 makes clear,

**Meditate on
1 Corinthians 1:30.**
What are the three qualities listed here that you have gained through your union with Jesus?

this has enormous implications for your spiritual life. In Christ your old, sinful way of living has been crucified and you have been resurrected with him into a new life. You don't have to be preoccupied any more with things you did in the past. You have been set free from slavery to sin (verse 6). You have received a new nature which enables you to overcome sin. In Christ you are *dead* to sin and *alive* to God (verse 11). No longer does your heavenly Father see you in the tattered rags of your own sinful rebellion. Instead he sees you "in Christ." Your identity now springs from your living union with the Son of God.

"We haven't been eliminated in this union," writes Robin Boisvert, "but Christ has been added...We haven't been handed a guide book and told to find our way to heaven. Instead, we've been given a Guide who will escort us there personally."[10]

> **"** It is only because of our preassigned union with Christ from before the creation of the world that all the blessings of salvation eventually come to us. Here at the very beginning all human merit is excluded. To God be all the praise![11] **"**
>
> **—Anthony Hoekema**

Why is God delighted to be with you during your daily devotions? Because you are in Christ. Why does he forgive you when you sin? Because you are in Christ. Why will he never leave you nor forsake you? Why has he taken responsibility to lead you in his good and perfect will? Why does he bless you with every spiritual blessing? Why can you rest securely in his love? Because of the initiative he has taken to unite you forever to his perfect Son, Jesus Christ!

4 Who came up with the motto, "United We Stand, Divided We Fall"?

(Answer printed upside down at the bottom of the next page)

❑ Two-time presidential candidate H. Ross Perot

❑ The AFL-CIO

❑ American colonists protesting British rule

❑ Finalists at the National Three-Legged Race Relays

❑ President Lincoln, just before the Civil War

❑ Organizers of the Women's Temperance Movement

❑ Two criminals preparing their alibi

#7: Cleansed by God

If I were reading Paul's statement in Romans 6 for the first time, I can pretty well predict the response I would give at this point: "Freed from sin? *Me?* Remind me of that the next time I slice my first shot off the tee, or get rear-ended in traffic. I'm not exactly perfect, you know."

How true. Even though our union with Jesus gives us power to overcome sin, we still wallow in plenty of muck. That's why it's so important that we understand the gracious fact of God's forgiveness:

> Once you were alienated from God and were enemies in your minds because of your evil behavior. But now he has reconciled you by Christ's physical body through death to present you holy in his sight, without blemish and free from accusation. (Colossians 1:21-22)

One of the first Bible verses I memorized as a new Christian was 1 John 1:9: "If we confess our sins, he is faithful and just and will forgive us our sins and purify us from all unrighteousness." By his death on the Cross, Jesus purchased your forgiveness. He has paid the price for all your sin—past, present, and future. Take confidence in your merciful God, who says, "I, even I, am he who blots out your transgressions, for my own sake, and remembers your sins no more" (Isaiah 43:25).

For Further Study:
When God forgives you, what does he do with your sins? (See Psalm 103:3, Isaiah 38:17, and Micah 7:19)

In addition to being forgiven, you have been *justified* by God. This is a very important word, so think hard with me for a minute. Justification means God has declared you righteous, just as if you had never sinned. He's thrown away all your old files. He has canceled your debt. As incredible as it seems (and totally undeserved), he now sees you the same way he sees his Son. Through justification, God has imputed the perfect, spotless righteousness of Jesus Christ to you. How can he do that? Why would he view you as righteous even though your actions are still "shot through with sin"? For one reason only—because you are in Christ.

#8: Changed by God

Before starting this book, did you realize how much God had done in you and for you? You have been totally transformed! Once you were dead in sin and doomed to eternal destruction. Now you're alive in Christ and destined to

Answer to Question 4 from page 11: American colonists protesting British rule. The same could be said about our union with Christ. But by God's grace, we don't have to worry about ever being separated from him (Romans 8:38-39).

spend eternity in the glorious presence of God. That's no small change, as the Bible explains: "Therefore, if anyone is in Christ, he is a new creation; the old has gone, the new has come! All this is from God, who reconciled us to himself through Christ" (2 Corinthians 5:17-18).

Most Christians are happy just to know God has taken away their sins. But that's only half of the good news. Not only has something been taken away—something has been added as well! Because you are now united with Christ, his divine nature is in you.

> His divine power has given us everything we need for life and godliness, through our knowledge of him who called us by his own glory and goodness. Through these he has given us his very great and precious promises, so that through them you may participate in the divine nature and escape the corruption in the world caused by evil desires. (2 Peter 1:3-4)

That's what you call CHANGE!

Since we've covered a lot of ground in this first study, let's close with a quick review. Before God had even created the world, he *chose* you to be his child. He was intimately involved in *creating* you according to his own unique design. But your *condition* alienated you from God; you were dead in sin, unable to save yourself or even seek God. Then, in an act of infinite, undeserved mercy, God *called* you to himself by the gospel and made you spiritually alive through regeneration.

> **"** It is not that we haven't sinned or, as Christians, do not continue to sin. We know we sin daily—in fact, many times a day. Even as Christians our best efforts are still marred with imperfect performance and impure motives. But God no longer 'sees' either our deliberate disobedience or our marred performances. Instead He 'sees' the righteousness of Christ, which He has already imputed to us.[12] **"**
>
> **—Jerry Bridges**

You responded to his call through *conversion* when you put your trust in Christ (faith) and began a life of submitted obedience (repentance). Now you are *in Christ,* united with him forever. God has justified you and *cleansed* you from the stain of sin. And because of God's work in you, you have been dramatically *changed.* You are a new creation!

Once you were spiritually dead; now you are spiritually alive. Once you were an enemy of God; now he has made you his friend. Once you were incapable of pleasing God; now his divine power is at work in you, helping you triumph over sin. At every point God has taken the initiative

Meditate on Colossians 1:13-14.
God has freed you from the Devil's dungeon and transferred your citizenship to the kingdom of his Son. Can you think of a bigger (and better) change than that?

13

to accomplish your salvation! Remember that the next time you sin. Remember that when life's waves crash against you with pulverizing force. Remember that and be at peace, knowing your Creator and Savior holds you eternally in his hand. ∎

Repentance = Process of Change = ~~Fruit~~ Fruit
(confession)

GROUP DISCUSSION

1. What is one thing you do *really* well? What is one thing you couldn't do if your life depended on it?

2. What motivated God to choose you?

3. Would you be willing to share your answer to Question 2 on page 5?

4. Does the Bible's description of the human condition surprise you? Offend you?

5. What happened to make you spiritually alive?

6. Describe two ways in which God's initiative requires your cooperation. (Pages 8-9)

7. Can you think of a few ways your life would change if you were suddenly "united" to a billionaire?

8. What does God see when he views your sins? (Page 12)

9. Who has the stronger grip—you or God?

RECOMMENDED READING

This Great Salvation by Robin Boisvert and C.J. Mahaney (Gaithersburg, MD: People of Destiny International, 1992)

How Can I Be Sure I'm a Christian? by Donald Whitney (Colorado Springs, CO: NavPress, 1994)

Chosen by God by R.C. Sproul (Wheaton, IL: Tyndale House Publishers, 1986)

The Christian Life: A Doctrinal Introduction by Sinclair Ferguson (Carlisle, PA: The Banner of Truth Trust, 1989)

Answers to Warm-Up (from page 1): **Ben Franklin** was the first head of the U.S. Post Office; *The Adventures of Tom Sawyer* by Mark Twain was the first type-written novel; **Wyoming** first acknowledged a woman's right to vote; and **A & P** was the first U.S. chain store. (Source: *Disney Adventures*, January '95)

NO OTHER BOOK LIKE IT

BIBLE STUDY 2 Timothy 3:16-17

WARM-UP To test whether an ancient book has been accurately translated over the centuries, historians compare the modern translation with early manuscripts of the same work. The greater the number of manuscripts, the more reliable the modern translation. On that basis, which of the following works would be considered most reliable?

A. Homer's *The Iliad*

B. Thucydides' *History*

C. *The New Testament*

D. Caesar's *The Gallic War*

E. Dr. Suess' *The Cat in the Hat*

(See page 27 for answer)

PERSONAL STUDY As we saw in the previous study, God saved you by touching the hard, dead core of your spirit and bringing you to life. Being born again is the greatest miracle you will ever experience. It certainly won't be the last supernatural event of your life, but it will remain the most profound. All other spiritual experiences will be overshadowed by this climactic event.

Now that you are spiritually alive in Christ, you have a growing capacity to understand spiritual truth. You can now comprehend spiritual mysteries that once seemed irrelevant, or possibly even ridiculous, to you. God has begun revealing to you that the Bible is a *living* book… not in the sense that it will fetch the newspaper for you or pull up a chair at the kitchen table, but living in the sense that its words penetrate deep into your heart and address specific issues in your life.

> **When the believer opens the Bible, it is with the profound and solemn conviction that he is about to listen to the voice of God![1]**
>
> —Octavius Winslow

Every new Christian should have an increasing hunger to know the content of the Bible. It is written, "Man does not live on bread alone, but on every word that comes from the mouth of God" (Matthew 4:4). As you study God's Word, you will find that it refocuses your view of God, of yourself, and of others. In fact, it will begin to shape your entire life. Like a master road map, it will begin directing the steps you take. It will begin changing the attitudes of your heart, the words of your mouth, and the priorities that govern your life.

You will find that this living Word knows more about you than you know about yourself. Not only will it teach you about who you are, but it will also reveal the multifaceted nature of the God you serve.

Not Magic, but...

Many view the Bible as a list of "do's and don'ts." What a sadly distorted view of this magnificent book! The Bible contains the very words of Almighty God. It has been preserved through the centuries as his primary means for communicating to his people. When followers of Christ read the Bible, the Holy Spirit speaks through it and impresses its content on our hearts. God's Word guides, heals, comforts, confronts, encourages, warns, convicts, and changes us in order to make us like Jesus.

Apart from a diligent diet of God's Word, true spiritual progress is impossible. Every lasting spiritual breakthrough you ever experience will depend on having your mind renewed with God's thoughts, which are contained in his Word (Romans 12:2). Do not be overwhelmed at how much you do not know. Do not be concerned about sections that are confusing or difficult for you to understand. At this point, rejoice that you hold in your hand a book made of paper, leather, ink, and glue that—when studied with a humble and teachable heart—comes alive with relevant answers and guidance for your life.

For Further Study:
Read Psalm 19:7-11. See how many benefits of Scripture you can find in this passage.

The Bible is your key to becoming what God wants you to be. Not only will it show you what to do (and what not to do), but it will create within you a desire for the very things it requires! Better yet, by hiding God's word in your heart (Psalm 119:11), you will be empowered to act on those desires—to develop a brand-new set of habits and thoughts that please God.

---

1 It's 6:15 on a Thursday morning…you've just read a verse in your Bible that is *totally* confusing. What should you do?

❑ Assume God is telling you to go back to bed

❑ Drink several cups of coffee

❑ Ask God for insight and continue with your reading

❑ Try to find "Dial-a-Pastor" in your Yellow Pages

❑ Look for a Marvel Comics version of the Scriptures

These last few paragraphs almost sound like I'm describing a magic wand, don't they? The Bible isn't magic, but it *is* supernaturally powerful, and we must approach it with an attitude of reverence (Isaiah 66:2). For as we digest its teaching, as we yield our minds and wills to its truth, a mysterious transformation begins to occur—we begin reflecting the image of Jesus Christ.

Last year, more Bibles were sold than any other book in the world. The same was true five years ago. Fifteen years ago. Fifty years ago. In fact, the Bible is the top-selling book of all time, and reaffirms that rank every year. What book has been translated into over 1,500 languages? The Bible. And why? Because millions have discovered what you will discover as well: that God's Word powerfully transforms the lives of those who come to it hungry for real truth…and ready for lasting change.

What the Bible Says About the Bible

Can you imagine driving in a country that had no traffic laws? It would be a disaster! With nothing but their own instincts to guide them, drivers would be lucky to make it more than a block or two without getting demolished.

Every 16-year-old needs a driver's manual to learn how to survive on the highways. Likewise, every Christian needs the Bible to live the Christian life. It lays out the parameters. It sets the standards. God's Word is to have complete and final authority in every area of your life. You certainly can't steer your life by the signposts of modern

Meditate on Psalm 119:105. Without the Bible to guide you, you're blind!

culture. All that a Christian thinks, says, and does should be governed by God's Word.

Unless you have grown up in an environment where the Bible was respected and obeyed, you may find these last few statements a bit shocking. You may even be thinking to yourself, *Why? What qualifies the Bible to be the final authority in my life?* It's a good question. As we look for an answer, let's let the Bible speak for itself.

The Bible is inspired by God. *"All Scripture is God-breathed and is useful for teaching, rebuking, correcting, and training in righteousness, so that the man of God may be thoroughly equipped for every good work" (2 Timothy 3:16-17).*

> **“** By the authority of the Bible we mean that the Bible, as the expression of God's will to us, possesses the right supremely to define what we are to believe and how we are to conduct ourselves.[2] **”**
>
> —**Millard Erickson**

The phrase "God-breathed" means that God, not man, brought this book into existence, even though he used human instruments. As John Stott has written, "He [God] took minds, pens, hearts, educations, tongues of men and inspired them to write exactly what he wanted to say." No other book can claim divine authorship. Every word from Genesis 1:1 to Revelation 22:21 is God's perfect, infallible word to mankind. This is what gives the Bible its authority.

The Bible is "living." *"For you have been born again, not of perishable seed, but of imperishable, through the living and enduring word of God" (1 Peter 1:23).*

Scripture is not some musty historical record of a God on the move in millennia past. It is a living document which speaks to God's people in every generation and culture. Though written thousands of years ago, the Bible's wisdom is timeless. It offers understanding and insight for every dilemma or challenge you will ever face. As you read it, the Holy Spirit will reveal things to you and help you apply it to your daily experience.

It was said of Moses that he "received *living words* to pass on to us" (Acts 7:38). His words, and all the other words in the Bible, still live and speak to us today.

The Bible is penetratingly powerful. *"The word of God is living and active. Sharper than any double-edged sword, it penetrates even to dividing soul and spirit, joints and marrow; it judges the thoughts and attitudes of the heart" (Hebrews 4:12).*

God's Word has no peer. It has no rival. It far surpasses any other piece of literature or body of knowledge. Of all

For Further Study:
According to 2 Peter 1:20-21, what is the origin of Scripture?

18

For Further Study:
What do the descriptions of God's Word in Jeremiah 23:29 tell you about its power?

the "double-edged swords" man has devised—the sword of humanistic philosophy, the sword of psychology, the sword of rationalism, or even the sword of Ann Landers—none can pierce and change the heart like the Bible can.

Scripture is sufficient for handling every situation. Nothing else provides the moral guidelines, the practical wisdom, the hope, or the food for man's soul like God's Word. It comforts the widow, convicts the sinner, imparts wisdom for the parent, reconciles husbands and wives, encourages the desperate, heals the sick, and strengthens the weary. God's Word is sharper than *any* double-edged sword and it cuts deeply into every possible condition humanity will ever face.

The Bible is flawless. *"As for God his way is perfect; the word of the Lord is flawless" (Psalm 18:30).*

Scripture contains no errors, and it doesn't contradict itself. Greater than the greatest literature, it is flawless communication from its Author to his audience. God's Word does not capitulate to man's evaluation; rather, it evaluates man. Every part of man. And the assessments it makes are accurate in every detail.

The Bible is above all things. *"I will bow down toward your holy temple and will praise your name for your love and your faithfulness, for you have exalted above all things your name and your word" (Psalm 138:2).*

God's Word seeks counsel from no one. It needs no human approval or endorsement. People may disagree with it, hate it, ignore it, or burn it, but that does not jeopardize its authority in the slightest.

Meditate on Luke 21:33. The Bible's truth will never be contradicted by scientific developments, cultural shifts, or archaeological findings. It will stand forever!

Man's opinion of God's Word is totally irrelevant, for it is God, not man, who has elevated Scripture above all things. He has established his Word as central and supreme. God's Word will accomplish all he has decreed (Isaiah 55:11). Though many have challenged and mocked it over the centuries, God's Word towers over the paltry objections of its challengers. Scripture will abide forever, and not one word of it will pass away. We do well to approach it reverently, submitting to its wisdom and feasting on its wonderful revelations of God.

2 The only appropriate response to Scripture can be described in one word. What is it? (See Isaiah 66:2)

19

Studying as if Your Life Depended On It

I live in Virginia Beach, where our local newspaper regularly runs fishing reports. One September it reported an eerie event that occurred off the coast of North Carolina. The story went like this.

A charter boat had been fishing for blue marlin and finally hooked one. A big one. Breaking the calm, one of the reels began making the unmistakable "ziiiing" everybody had been waiting for. The first mate sprang into action, coaching the novice fisherman as the marlin slashed and fought frantically to shake itself free.

For two hours the 700-pound fish and the 60-foot boat were locked in a battle of wills off the continental shelf. Finally the giant marlin surfaced, exhausted, and floated quietly on its side. Every ounce of fight was drained from its majestic body. But neither the peaceful blue skies nor the 2,000-foot deep indigo water gave any indication of what was to follow.

The first mate, who had witnessed this drama dozens of times, routinely grabbed the line and began maneuvering the fish into position to haul it aboard. He knew the proper technique was to wrap the line *once* around his gloved hand and forearm. That way, if the marlin gave a sudden jerk, he could loosen his grip and the line would slide harmlessly off his arm. But this time, for some unknown reason, the mate wrapped the line *twice* around his arm.

With an unexpected, violent thrash of its powerful tail, the marlin made a final effort to jerk free. The line knotted around the mate's wrist. In an instant he was yanked overboard. Horrified, the rest of the fishing party watched as the giant fish swam casually down into the depths, pulling the first mate behind him.

He was never seen again.

The first mate paid a horrible price for not doing his job the way it should have been done. Landing a panic-stricken, 700-pound fish is not something you should approach carelessly. The same goes for the Christian life. Attempting to live for Christ without a steady diet of God's Word is flirting with serious danger.

How should you approach the Word of God? As if your life depends on it—because it does. I recommend the "RTAMMA" approach: Read, Think, Ask, Memorize, Meditate, and Apply. It's not much of an acronym, but it may help you remember the six steps necessary for getting the most out of Scripture.

For Further Study:
Read Deuteronomy 32:45-47. How did Moses describe God's laws to the people of Israel? Can you see your need to treat Scripture with this same respect?

Read. You can't benefit from the Bible without reading it. That's pretty obvious. But in order to read it effectively, you've got to slow down and interact with it. Set aside time in your day to read a couple of chapters in an unhurried way, slowly bathing your mind with truth. Turn off the stereo. Stop daydreaming about next week's hunting trip with Uncle Louie or the Grand Opening Sale at the new discount mall. Focus on listening to God speak to you through his Word.

For most of us, early morning is the most practical time to read. This requires going to bed early enough so you can wake up clear-headed and not be comatose. (Notice how God's Word is already affecting your lifestyle? When it is the passion and priority of your life, it even affects your bedtime!)

> ❝ Let us read the Bible reverently and diligently, with an honest determination to believe and practice all we find in it. It is no light matter how we use this book.[3] ❞
>
> **—J.C. Ryle**

Though the entire Bible is God's inspired Word, new Christians should choose their diet carefully. Many start off fast in Genesis, only to die a slow death midway through Leviticus. One way to add variety is to read a chapter from the historical or prophetic books of the Old Testament, then a chapter from the poetic books (Job, Psalms, or Proverbs), followed by a chapter in the New Testament. An average reader like myself can do all this in 20 minutes. Another option is to go chapter by chapter through a particular book of the Bible.

Systematically working through the Scriptures is vital for spiritual growth. Excuses abound why we can't or don't, but…how can I say this tactfully?…they are all bogus. You always find time to do what's important to you.

My wife Janis jogs almost every day. How does she find the time? She doesn't—she *makes* time, because jogging is important to her. Why do I only jog once or twice a year? Because it is important to me to *avoid* jogging.

Meditate on 1 Timothy 4:7-8. Your spirit won't naturally enjoy exercise—you need to get it in shape!

Golf, on the other hand, is serious business. I always find several slivers of time each summer to hack around a golf course. By now you know why: because it is important to me. (It is my form of aerobic exercise.) Janis, however, has never played golf in her life. And she shows no signs of starting any time soon.

If we want to grow as Christians, we need to *make* time to read the Bible faithfully. Otherwise, says author Donald Whitney, "we severely restrict the main flow of God's sanctifying grace toward us."[4]

3 How often do you read the Bible? Check one of the boxes below to see how your Bible reading habits compare with those of the average American.

❏ **Daily** (11%)   ❏ **2–3 times a week** (9%)

❏ **Weekly** (13%)   ❏ **2–3 times a month** (6%)

❏ **Once a month** (8%)   ❏ **Occasionally** (26%)

❏ **Never** (22%)   ❏ **Can't say** (5%)

Percentages indicate number of Americans polled who gave each response. Source: George Gallup, Jr. and Sarah Jones, *100 Questions and Answers: Religion In America* (Princeton, NJ: Princeton Religion Research Center, 1989), p. 40.

Think. Sometimes I reach the end of a Bible passage and realize I have been thinking about every conceivable thing under the sun except what I was reading. I have spent times of Bible study planning a fishing trip with my boys, or mentally fine-tuning my backswing, or worse! When this happens (and it inevitably will), it is best to pause for a moment and ask God to help you focus your thoughts. Then, force your renegade mind to think about what's on the page.

Ask. When I receive a personal letter, I instinctively want to know, "Who is this from?" The second question that comes to mind is, "What is going on in this person's life that prompted him or her to write?" Asking questions like these during Bible study will help you immensely in grasping the deeper spiritual truths of a passage. Who is the author? Who is the audience? What is the cultural and historical setting of this particular book? What does the passage tell you about yourself, about God, or about some biblical truth? A good study Bible will answer many of these questions in its introductory or study notes. Other helpful study tools would include a concordance, a Bible dictionary, and a Bible atlas.

Memorize. I am amazed at how many people say they can't memorize Scripture. These are the folks who can recite verbatim the entire roster of their favorite baseball team, the phone numbers of all their friends, ingredients and measurements for 20 different recipes, or the days, times, and channels of their favorite TV shows. But when it comes to memorizing God's Word, they are convinced they have the brainpower of pea soup.

When it comes to memorizing Scripture, the issue is not ability but motivation. Let me illustrate.

Meditate on Psalm 119:97. Does this reflect your feelings about God's Word?

For Further Study:
What do you think it means to write truth "on the tablet of your heart"? (Proverbs 3:3) How can Scripture memorization accomplish this?

One day I was trying to help my children learn some Bible verses. They looked at me as if I had just asked them to go over Niagara Falls in a bathtub. They were convinced it was too hard. So I made each of them a deal. In order to get their allowance, they would need to memorize at least three verses of my choice per week. Otherwise, they would miss out.

Within two or three days they had the verses memorized by heart and could recite them perfectly. Hmmmmm… This led me to a couple of conclusions. First, my children *could* handle the brain strain of memorizing Scripture. Second, I was headed toward personal bankruptcy.

I periodically jot verses on a 3 x 5 card and review them throughout the day. Janis will often post verses next to the kitchen sink so she can glance at them as she works. This simple discipline is a great way to inscribe God's Word on your mind and heart.

Meditation. As important as these first four steps are for absorbing God's Word, nothing packs the spiritual wallop of meditation. Think carefully about this quote from Charles Spurgeon, the British pastor who captivated thousands with his preaching during the mid-1800s:

> 66 Regardless of how busy we become with all things Christian, we must remember that the most transforming practice available to us is the disciplined intake of Scripture.[5] 99
>
> —**Donald Whitney**

Our lives are not nourished merely by listening awhile to this, and then to that, and then to the other part of divine truth. Hearing, reading, marking, and learning, all require inwardly digesting to complete their usefulness, and the inward digesting of the truth lies for the most part in meditating upon it. Why is it that some Christians, although they hear many sermons, make but slow advances in the divine life? Because they neglect their closets, and do not thoughtfully meditate on God's Word.[6]

Biblical meditation has nothing to do with Buddhist shrines and saffron robes. The word meditation simply means to "talk to oneself," or to reflect on a thought. Think of a cow repeatedly chewing its cud—that's what your brain does when you meditate on something.

People meditate all the time without realizing it. They meditate on the paper they are trying to write by semester's end. They meditate on next week's board meeting or the cost of installing new kitchen cabinets.

I've seen people at stoplights jabbering to themselves about something so consuming, they just had to talk about it!

Meditation is work—exhausting work at times. Why? Because your mind tends to be the most undisciplined part of you. Yet God still commands Christians to meditate on his Word. Reflect on the following comment by John Flavel, a Puritan pastor who lived in the 16th century:

> **4** Remember, it is not hasty reading, but serious meditating upon holy and heavenly truths, that make them prove sweet and profitable to the soul...It is not he that reads most, but he that meditates most, that will prove the choicest, sweetest, wisest and strongest Christian.[7] **77**
>
> —**Thomas Brooks**

We have a deep distaste for meditation. This is not a matter of temperament. The recluse or introvert has no advantage over the active, busy Christian. True meditation is a work to which we are all naturally indisposed, but it is one to which the Holy Spirit prompts those whom he indwells, those who have trusted Christ. To the work of meditation...believers must apply themselves; but first they must recognize it as a duty and understand what it involves.[8]

Think about Scripture. Memorize it. Say it over and over to yourself. Emphasize different parts of a verse and consider the various shades of meaning that surface. For instance, you might meditate on Psalm 1:2 like this:

"But his **delight** is in the law of the Lord..."

Why "delight" and not some other word? What does it mean to delight in something? What do I delight in?

"But his delight is in the **law** of the Lord..."

How could a law be delightful? What's my attitude toward the law?

"But his delight is in the law of the **Lord**..."

What does the title "Lord" imply? How well do I respond to human authority? To God's authority?

Meditate on Psalm 1:1-3. What is the man in this passage known for? What are the results?

Ponder the text. Chew on it. Extract from it the priceless insights that feed and inspire your soul. If you wish to benefit from the spiritual discipline of meditation, here are the requirements: a will submitted to God's Word, a heart hungry for all God says, and a mind focused on the passage at hand.

4 If you were a Hindu, you would meditate in order to *empty* your mind. How would you describe the goal of Christian meditation?

Application. The last and often most neglected part of Bible study is application. "Like chewing without swallowing," writes Donald Whitney, "so meditation is incomplete without some type of application…If we don't apply those verses to life they won't be of much more lasting value to us than they are to [a] parrot."[9]

You can't grow strong as a Christian unless you learn to apply God's Word to your life. Application, not just information, should always be your ultimate objective when studying the Scripture.

For Further Study: For a description of someone who listens to the Word without applying it, read James 1:22-25.

One of the most effective ways to apply Scripture is to interact with it in a question-and-answer format. Let's close by entering into a dialogue with the two verses that undergird this entire study:

> All Scripture is God-breathed and is useful for teaching, rebuking, correcting and training in righteousness, so that the man of God may be thoroughly equipped for every good work. (2 Timothy 3:16-17)

Does this passage show me something about God?

It sure does. He has personally "breathed" Scripture into being. He has given me a resource that's practical. And he is concerned about the effect of his Word on me.

Does this passage show me something about myself?

Righteousness doesn't just happen—I must be trained in it. That training will involve rebuking and correcting. Am I willing to pay that price for righteousness? Am I yielded to Scripture's teaching and convinced that it is God-breathed? If so, I can look forward to being "equipped for every good work"—what potential! My life isn't meaningless. God has work for me to do!

Does this passage tell me to stop doing something or start doing something?

> **❝** If the Bible were the most boring book in the world, dull, uninteresting and seemingly irrelevant, it would still be our duty to study it. If its literary style were awkward and confusing, the duty would remain. We live as human beings under an obligation by divine mandate to study diligently God's Word. He is our Sovereign, it is his Word and he commands that we study it.[10] **❞**
>
> —**R.C. Sproul**

It shows me four specific uses for the Bible: teaching, rebuking, correcting, and training in righteousness. Do I know what these things mean? Am I doing them? This passage also tells me to be *thoroughly* equipped for every good work. What's my current status? In what areas am I ill-equipped? What parts of Scripture should I be studying in order to become better equipped?

There are many other questions you could ask yourself after studying these two verses. It takes time and thought, but this active dialogue with Scripture will transform your Bible study from a tedious chore into a daily adventure. Application is essential, for only then is real spiritual growth occurring. Only then is measurable change taking place. Only then is God's Word having the impact on your life he intends for it to have. ■

GROUP DISCUSSION

1. What were your impressions of the Bible before you became a Christian?

2. If the Bible is God's "primary means for communicating to his people" (Page 16), what are some other means?

3. Can you recall a time when God's Word guided you through a specific situation or decision?

4. Has it ever seemed like a particular verse of the Bible "leaped out at you"? Describe your experience to the group.

5. What part of the Bible are you reading currently? When do you read? Do you have a favorite reading spot?

6. Are there tips you could share with the group that have made your own Bible study more consistent or profitable?

7. As a group, pick any passage of Scripture and spend five minutes asking questions about it. (See page 25)

8. Are you willing to live under the authority of Scripture?

RECOMMENDED READING

Spiritual Disciplines for the Christian Life by Donald Whitney (Colorado Springs, CO: NavPress, 1991)

How to Read the Bible for All It's Worth by Gordon Fee and Douglas Stuart (Grand Rapids, MI: Zondervan Publishing House, 1982)

Knowing Scripture by R.C. Sproul (Downers Grove, IL: InterVarsity Press, 1977)

Answer to Warm-Up
(from page 15): C.) *The New Testament*, which is supported by more than 20,000 early manuscripts. Compare that with *The Iliad*, which has 643 supporting manuscripts—the most of any other piece of ancient literature. (Source: *More Than A Carpenter*, by Josh McDowell, Tyndale House Publishers, Wheaton, IL, 1977)

STUDY THREE

WHAT A WONDERFUL GOD YOU ARE!

BIBLE STUDY Colossians 1:9-14

WARM-UP If you're a mathematics buff, you know the value of pi (π) is roughly 3.14159. However, its exact value cannot be determined. Can you guess the number of decimal places to which the value of pi has been calculated?

A. 620 places after the decimal point

B. 16,167 places after the decimal point

C. 8,388,576 places after the decimal point

D. 51,539,600,000 places after the decimal point

E. Unless it's apple or cherry pie, I'm not interested

(See page 40 for answer)

PERSONAL STUDY I once read a story about a mother of eight who lived in rural Maryland. One day she came home from the grocery store and saw five of the children in the yard. She could tell they were fascinated by something.

As she watched, she suddenly discovered the source of their excitement. Some wild baby skunks had wandered from the fields into their yard, and the children had them cornered. Mom was appalled. They were cute little fur-balls, but she knew they were "fully equipped."

At the top of her voice she screamed, "Children, run!"

The children immediately sensed their mom's panic. Though they couldn't see any danger, they knew they had to hightail it out of there. So each kid grabbed a skunk and ran![1]

Misunderstandings can be costly. In this case, the stench eventually wore off and the family could laugh about the experience. The consequences are far more serious, however, when someone misunderstands the nature of God.

29

Many do. If you asked 100 people at the Los Angeles International Airport to describe God, you would get an incredible spectrum of answers. Some would say he is a cosmic killjoy, ready to zap anyone who cracks a smile. Others would describe him as a syrupy grandpa. Most would distort the picture in one way or another, depending on their own beliefs and experiences.

One thing would be true for all these people: Whether they realize it or not, their understanding (or misunderstanding) of God controls them. It is constantly influencing their decisions and motivating their actions. The same is true of you.

> ❝ The foundation of all true knowledge of God must be a clear mental apprehension of his perfections as revealed in Holy Scripture. An unknown God can neither be trusted, served, nor worshipped.[2] ❞
>
> —A.W. Pink

Nothing affects your daily life more than your view of God. As A.W. Tozer has written, "What comes into our minds when we think about God is the most important thing about us."[3]

A disciple will become like his master. *Developing an accurate picture of God will profoundly influence your growth as a Christian.* That's why you must learn of him. Hunger after him. Make finding out what kind of God he really is the supreme passion of your life.

Meditate on Matthew 11:28-30. Here's one invitation you wouldn't want to turn down!

Thankfully you don't need a Gallup Poll to figure out the nature of God. He has revealed himself fully in the Scripture, and he wants to be found by you as you seek him with all your heart (Jeremiah 29:13-14). Let's turn now to his flawless, reliable Word and begin developing a clear picture of this wonderful God you serve.

An Eternal God

Scripture's first clue to the nature of God shows that he is eternal: "In the beginning, God…" (Genesis 1:1). Here in the first sentence of the Bible we find that God predates time. He had no beginning. Before the beginning began, God was.

It is impossible to imagine an eternal and self-existent God. He has never matured, grown, improved, or increased. He is no older now than he was one thousand years ago. God is today what he has always been and always will be. He is "the same yesterday and today and forever" (Hebrews 13:8). Though it may scramble your brain, let it strengthen your heart: God is eternal!

1 Which of the following, in your opinion, most closely approximates eternity?

❏ An average wait at your doctor's office

❏ The time it takes the IRS to mail your tax refund

❏ The Friday afternoon before your two-week vacation

❏ The length of a single contraction during childbirth

❏ The time it takes a child to eat one serving of spinach

An Infinite God

Think for a moment about the size of the universe. The sun is a star big enough to contain 1.3 million planets the size of Earth. And yet it is just one among 100 billion stars astronomers estimate to be in our galaxy.

The Milky Way galaxy is 600,000 trillion miles across. It would take a light beam 100,000 years (traveling at 186,282 miles per second) to cross the entire expanse. But the Milky Way is only an average-sized galaxy, one among millions (perhaps billions) in a universe scientists say is still expanding.

> ❝ God's center is everywhere, his circumference nowhere.[4] ❞
> —**Thomas Watson**

Our universe is colossal… yet God holds it all in his hand. The Bible says Jesus "ascended higher than all the heavens, in order to fill the whole universe" (Ephesians 4:10). God is limitless. He is beyond measure. He cannot be contained and he has no boundaries. He is totally incomprehensible. This should not intimidate you from seeking to know him, but it should keep you in a constant state of awe:

For Further Study: Read Ephesians 1:22-23. Stretch your brain for a minute by thinking about what it means to serve a God who "fills everything in every way."

Although God reveals himself as a personal being capable of fellowship with man, whom we can worship and love, and to whom we can pray with the assurance of being heard and answered; nevertheless he fills heaven and earth; he is exalted above all we can know or think. He is infinite in his being and perfections.[5]

At the outer edges of the universe, where even man's most powerful telescopes can't see, is God—sustaining and surpassing it all.

A Loving God

Nowhere is the magnitude of God's nature more apparent than in his love. His love is constant, overwhelming, and totally undeserved. There is nothing a Christian could ever do to earn or increase God's infinite love. "We may force God to punish us," wrote Thomas Watson, "but not to love us."[6] His love sought us out even though we hated him and rebelled against his commands.

The apostle Paul knew how it felt to be apprehended by God's love. While on his way to persecute Christians, this devout Jew was himself overcome by the life-changing love of Jesus. From then on, one of his main concerns for the churches was that they grasp how wide and long and high and deep was the love of God, and *know* this love that surpasses knowledge (Ephesians 3:18-19). Paul wanted them to embrace this wonderful truth. To be overwhelmed by it. To revel in the boundless ocean of God's love.

> ### "THE LOVE OF GOD"
> #### (1917)
>
> The love of God is greater far
> Than tongue or pen can ever tell.
> It goes beyond the highest star
> And reaches to the lowest hell.
> The guilty pair bowed down with care
> God gave his Son to win.
> His erring child he reconciled
> And pardoned from his sin.
> O love of God, how rich and pure,
> How measureless and strong;
> It shall forevermore endure—
> The saints' and angels' song.
>
> **—Lyrics by F.M. Lehman**

Human love is fickle. It ebbs and flows and has strings attached. But God's love is constant and inexhaustible. As Psalm 136 says over and over, "His love endures forever." Does God care for us because we are so endearing? I'm afraid not. "Mercy is not the fruit of our goodness, but the fruit of God's goodness."[7] Even when we have the dung of sin all over us, God's love still pours down over our lives, simply because he has chosen us and made a lasting covenant of love with us. He has no reason to love us except that which he keeps hidden deep in his own infinite heart.

You may face circumstances that tempt you to question the love of God. It could be a child with a lingering illness, or an inability to have children at all. A friend may slash you to pieces with vicious words. You might lose your job. But when the proverbial spaghetti of your life hits the fan and you're tempted to wonder, *Where is God? Where is his unfailing love?*, remember this: God's love has not changed. God's love toward you has not fluctuated. You may not understand why things are unfolding as they are, but you can rest in the knowledge that God's love endures forever.

Meditate on 2 Timothy 2:13. How does God treat those who are unfaithful in their love toward him?

An All-Knowing God

There are certain things God has never done. He has never asked angelic assistants to brief him on the state of the universe, or check the background of some new convert. God has never learned one micron of data. He doesn't need to—he knows all things. His knowledge is infinite and complete. And his memory is unlimited. Every speck of knowledge in the realms of medicine, oceanography, physics, history, astronomy, and all other fields is known by the One "in whom are hidden all the treasures of wisdom and knowledge" (Colossians 2:3).

God also has intimate knowledge of every person. Every thought, every motive, every secret longing of each human heart—God knows. "Nothing in all creation is hidden from God's sight," the Bible tells us. "Everything is uncovered and laid bare before the eyes of him to whom we must give account" (Hebrews 4:13). It wouldn't hurt to meditate on this the next time you're tempted to sin. God searches every nook and cranny of your life. "There is not the most subtle thought that comes into our mind," said Puritan pastor Thomas Watson, "but God perceives it."[8]

Sobering, isn't it? But serving an all-knowing God also brings tremendous security. Every problem his people face, every anxiety, every fear, God knows it all. Not only does he love you, but he knows every detail of every incident taking place in your life at this moment. Take comfort from this truth the next time you have too much month at the end of the money. Meditate on it as you are walking your feverish three-year-old up and down the hall at two o'clock in the morning. God knows your need. He knows your weakness. "For he knows how we are formed, he remembers that we are dust" (Psalm 103:14).

For Further Study:
Read Psalm 139:1-4. Judging by this passage, is there anything God *doesn't* know about you?

---

2 What's the most difficult situation in your life right now? As you describe it briefly in the space below, thank God that he knows and cares about every detail.

The moment something unpleasant or unexplainable happens to us, our first reaction is to question God. We assume he didn't *know* it was going to happen or he didn't *care* it was going to happen. But even those who know God is all-loving and all-knowing can succumb to the sin of doubting him. I proved it just recently.

On the way to my office one Saturday morning to finish this section on God's infinite knowledge, I stopped at the mall to buy a gift for some friends. While there I picked up a gift for me: a cinnamon bun and a 16-ounce cup of gourmet coffee. I have a special relationship with cinnamon buns, and the one I had picked out was the best of the batch. My coffee was so hot that a little whiff of steam curled out the tiny hole in the lid. By the time I got back to the car, I was salivating. I was tempted to speed just to get to my office and, uh, get to work.

> **"** We are all completely transparent before God. He sees and knows us totally. He knows every truth, even those not yet discovered by man, for it was he who built them into the creation.[9] **"**
> —**Millard Erickson**

But then it happened. As I made a left-hand turn, my coffee cup toppled out of its holder. I lunged for it in mid-flight while somehow managing to avoid an accident. But I only saved one swallow of the coffee, and had to watch as the rest oozed into the carpet.

What thoughts flashed instantaneously into my mind? "Lord, you *knew* how much that coffee meant to me! Why didn't you warn me so I could hold my cup and not have it spill all over my car? Certainly you know what it will taste like to wash down this cinnamon bun with cold water!" Yes, he knew. But he also knew how much coffee I had already slurped down that morning…any more and I might have banged my computer keys to pieces.

Meditate on Isaiah 40:27-31. Take hope in the Lord—he will never dismiss or overlook your needs.

From the silliest things, like losing a cup of coffee, to the trauma of burying a family member, God is intimately acquainted with all that goes on in our lives. Take refuge in that fact. When everything in you wants to scream out, "God, don't you see what I'm going through?", remember: Nothing escapes his watchful eye. "For a man's ways are in full view of the Lord, and he examines all his paths" (Proverbs 5:21). Again, we can learn from the wisdom of Thomas Watson: "God knows things past, present, and to come, *uno intuito*, at once; they are all before him in one entire prospect."[10] And because his infinite knowledge is equaled by infinite love, we can put our questions to rest.

A Wise God

You can feel Paul's excitement in Romans 11:33: "Oh, the depth of the riches of the wisdom and knowledge of God! How unsearchable his judgments, and his paths beyond tracing out!" But when you read between the lines of Paul's life—beatings, imprisonments, shipwrecks, and ultimately execution—his comments about God's wisdom take on a lot more significance. You see, Paul had learned that what is wise is not always fun.

Taking my three-year-old to the doctor for required shots is wise. When Madame X walks in the room with the needle, though, it is hardly fun, unless you enjoy trying to contain thirty-five pounds of twisting, flapping, flailing, screaming hysteria. When we're done, I'm the one in need of a sucker.

In his perfect wisdom, God will direct your life in ways you may never have chosen for yourself. His intent is to make you holy, not just happy. He wants to mold your character and conduct into the image of his Son. To accomplish that he will refine you through circumstances. Financial hardship. An overbearing boss. A broken relationship. God will use trials like these to expose your pride, selfishness, anger, or lack of self-control. It's wise…but not exactly fun. Kind of like booster shots.

The biblical character Job experienced incredible suffering and loss without ever fully understanding why. But in his agony he made this confession: "To God belong wisdom and power; counsel and understanding are his" (Job 12:13). Like Job, you can trust that God, in his wisdom, will only cause or allow that which contributes to the construction process of your life. J.I. Packer says it well:

> Increasing conformity to the image of Christ…is the sum and substance of the "good works" for which Christians have been created…Part of the answer to the question that life's roller coaster ride repeatedly raises, *why has this happened to me?*, is always: it is moral training and discipline, planned by my heavenly Father to help me forward along the path of Christ-like virtue.[11]

For Further Study: To understand one of God's reasons for letting us experience hardship, read Hebrews 12:5-11. If he didn't discipline us, he wouldn't love us.

A Sovereign God

During the 16th century, as the Reformation caused upheaval throughout Europe, Martin Luther made this jab at one of his strongest critics: "Erasmus, your thoughts of God are too human."[12] He could have been talking about any of us. We all have thoughts of God that are too human. We all want to bring God down to our level so we can deal with him on our terms. One long look at his sovereignty, however, should help us regain perspective.

Meditate on Isaiah 55:8-9. If your thoughts of God tend to be too human, read this!

Psalm 135:6 says, "The Lord does whatever pleases him, in the heavens and on the earth, in the seas and all their depths." God rules over all. Nothing threatens his kingly reign. Every atom must obey his command. He is the supreme ruler with all authority and power to accomplish his every decree. When he commands the Red Sea to divide and become dry ground so his people can cross over, it happens. When he declares a virgin's womb will bring forth a child, a Savior is born. When he commands the planets to orbit the sun, they do. When he commands the Berlin Wall to crumble, it disintegrates.

Some of today's top athletes brandish tattoos shaped like the "S" on Superman's chest. It's meant to be a statement of their skill or superiority. How senseless it must all appear to the Sovereign One who sits on the throne of the ages!

> He determines when, where, and under what circumstances each individual of our race is to be born, live, and die. Nations, no less than individuals, are thus in the hands of God, who assigns them their heritage in the earth, and controls their destiny.[13]

---

3 Suppose you were the most powerful ruler on earth, with all human authority at your disposal. Can you think of two or three things that would still be outside the bounds of your sovereignty?

-

-

-

Earlier we mentioned the sufferings of Job, a man head and shoulders above his peers in personal righteousness: "There is no one on earth like him; he is blameless and upright, a man who fears God and shuns evil" (Job 2:3). Yet Job experienced unbelievable agony—the loss of all his children, all his possessions, and finally his own health.

Meditate on Psalm 46:10. Even when God's plans don't seem to make any sense, you can trust that his sovereign purpose is right on schedule.

Why? Why would God subject such a good man to such horrible conditions? Job asked that question repeatedly. And he finally got his answer, though probably not the one he wanted.

You'll find God's response in chapters 38 through 41 of the Book of Job. Read them slowly. Meditate on them. But you may want to start by sitting down. For rather than justify himself by giving a reason for his actions, God returns Job's questions with a few questions of his own:

> Where were you when I laid the earth's foundation? Tell me, if you understand. Who marked off its dimensions? Surely you know! Who stretched a measuring line across it? … Can you bind the beautiful Pleiades? Can you loose the cords of Orion? Can you bring forth the constellations in their seasons or lead out the Bear with its cubs? Do you know the laws of the heavens? Can you set up God's dominion over the earth? (Job 38:4-5, 31-33)

After two chapters of this, Job is no longer asking any questions. But God continues, describing his absolute sovereignty over the universe and everything in it. When it's all over, Job is no longer shaking his fist at God in self-righteous indignation. Rather, he says, "I despise myself and repent in dust and ashes" (Job 42:6).

> ❝ Subject to none, influenced by none, absolutely independent, God does as he pleases, only as he pleases, always as he pleases. None can thwart him, none can hinder him.[14] ❞
>
> **—A.W. Pink**

God's love for Job never diminished for a second, and yet he allowed him to undergo trials of a magnitude you and I can hardly imagine. Why? Only God knows. "His sovereignty requires that he be absolutely free," writes A.W. Tozer, "which means simply that he must be free to do whatever he wills to do anywhere at any time to carry out his eternal purpose in every single detail without interference."[15] This was answer enough for Job. It will be for us, too, when God enables our hearts to accept it.

You won't have to study God's sovereignty long to realize who he is…and who you aren't. Even Nebuchadnezzar, the pagan king of Babylon, understood the difference: "All the peoples of the earth are regarded as nothing. He does as he pleases with the powers of heaven and the peoples of the earth. No one can hold back his hand or say to him: 'What have you done?'" (Daniel 4:35). God's rule is universal and eternal. He is worthy of all submission and honor.

You will never have every question answered. But you can trust that what God sovereignly allows in your life is the outworking of his infinite wisdom. What's unexplainable to you is no mystery to God. In his eternal plan, every circumstance—the joyful as well as the tragic—is helping conform you to the image of his Son, Jesus Christ. "For from him and through him and to him are all things. To him be the glory forever!" (Romans 11:36)

A Holy God

"Who among the gods is like you, O Lord? Who is like you—majestic in holiness, awesome in glory, working wonders?" (Exodus 15:11)

When Scripture calls God holy, it's underscoring the fact that he is infinitely greater than and distinct from his creation. None compares with him. None can comprehend his absolute purity and moral righteousness. None can fully understand his ways. "He is so far above and beyond us that he seems almost totally foreign to us," writes R.C. Sproul.[16] Consider just one example: While you and I sin constantly, God never sins. Never. Though Jesus faced every conceivable temptation during his earthly ministry, he yielded to none. And now he's not even tempted. (If that's not "totally foreign," what is?)

For Further Study:
What happens when you worship the Lord "in the splendor of his holiness"? (See Psalm 96:9)

The Bible tells us, "There is no one holy like the Lord" (1 Samuel 2:2). He dwells in "unapproachable light" (1 Timothy 6:16). Any illustration that would attempt to show the difference between God and man falls pitifully short. He is so different from us that, without his assistance, we cannot possibly comprehend it. But we can respond to it. Theologian Millard Erickson says a "proper reaction to God's holiness, his separateness, is one of awe, reverence, and silence."[17]

---

4 Does God's holiness have implications for your life? You bet it does! Look up 1 Peter 1:16, and write it in the space below.

God's holiness flavors all other aspects of his nature. You will never understand him properly if you overlook this truth. His love is a holy love, his wisdom is a holy wisdom, his power is a holy power, and his wrath is a holy wrath.

> **❝** God not only is personally free from any moral wickedness or evil. He is unable to tolerate the presence of evil. He is, as it were, allergic to sin and evil.[18] **❞**
>
> **—Millard Erickson**

Understanding God's holiness will comfort you, but it will trouble you at the same time. Think about it. Because he is holy, he will never lash out in human anger like we do. That is comforting. However, his holiness makes it impossible for him to overlook sin. He has a holy hatred toward evil. Sin is what nailed his innocent son Jesus to the Cross—how could he be indifferent toward it? He must deal with sin fairly or he ceases to be holy. That is troubling, because that means he must deal with *your* sin. All of it. Those who know the Holy One will never deal glibly with sin again.

Something to Boast About

A.W. Tozer's statement at the beginning of this study is no exaggeration: What comes to your mind when you think about God *is* the most important thing about you. That's why I encourage you to ponder his majesty. Meditate on the magnitude of his love, knowledge, wisdom, sovereignty, and holiness. And take to heart these words recorded by the prophet Jeremiah:

> "Let not the wise man boast of his wisdom or the strong man boast of his strength or the rich man boast of his riches, but let him who boasts boast about this: that he understands and knows me, that I am the Lord, who exercises kindness, justice and righteousness on earth, for in these I delight," declares the Lord. (Jeremiah 9:23-24)

I hope this study has given you a little more to boast about—not your I.Q. or your athletic achievements or your investment earnings, but your knowledge of God. There is so much to learn about our infinite, glorious Lord. Studying who he is, as we've done here, will deepen your affection for him. But now we turn to a study of what he has done—the great riches he has given you in Christ. And I expect that your boasting has only just begun. ■

1. How did you view God before you became a Christian?

2. What effect does it have on you to realize God knows every detail of your life?

3. The Bible says it's wrong to *doubt* God, but when trials come, do you think it's wrong to ask for an explanation?

4. God's intent "is to make you holy, not just happy" (page 35). Why is the distinction important?

5. Divide the group into two smaller groups. Let Group A discuss the question, "How would life be different if God were all-loving but not sovereign?" Have Group B discuss the question, "How would life be different if God were all-sovereign but not loving?" After five or ten minutes, compare your answers.

6. How might you evaluate whether someone is living a holy life? Give specifics.

7. Do you have any difficulty believing that God loves you?

8. Why are your thoughts of God the most important thing about you?

9. What was the most significant thing you learned in this study?

RECOMMENDED READING

Trusting God by Jerry Bridges (Colorado Springs, CO: NavPress, 1988)

The Pleasures of God by John Piper (Portland, OR: Multnomah Press, 1991)

Knowing God by J.I. Packer (Downers Grove, IL: InterVarsity Press, 1973)

The Attributes of God by A.W. Pink (Grand Rapids, MI: Baker Book House, 1975)

Answer to Warm-Up
(from page 29): D.) The value of π has been calculated to 51,539,600,000 places past the decimal point (as of July 6, 1997). 620 places was the record in 1946; 16,167 places in 1959; and 8,388,576 places in 1982. If this is what mathematicians do in their spare time, is it any wonder they have an unusual reputation? (Source: A Web site belonging to Simon Fraser University in British Columbia: http://www.cecm.sfu. ca/projects/ISC/ records.html

THE BIGGEST DECISION OF YOUR (NEW) LIFE

BIBLE STUDY John 7:37-39

WARM-UP Which of the following countries drinks the most Coca-Cola beverages *per capita* each year?

☐ Zimbabwe   ☐ Mexico

☐ China   ☐ Norway

☐ Australia   ☐ U.S.A.

☐ Israel   ☐ Russia

(See page 54 for answer)

PERSONAL STUDY One week after becoming a Christian, I desperately needed guidance. I wanted so much to make my life count for God. But how? Serving him was the least I could do after all he had done for me. What did he want me to do?

Maybe I should go to Africa and tell everyone about Jesus, I thought. (Africa was the toughest place I could imagine.) I pictured myself walking mile after dusty mile, knotty staff in hand, a parched prophet reduced to skin and bone. My cracked lips begged for a drop of relief. The red, sweat-soaked bandanna around my head did nothing to shield me from the heat as I heroically trekked across the desert plains looking for anyone who might not know Jesus. What would I eat? Roots? Bugs? What would I drink? How would I survive with the lions? Cheetahs? Hyenas? It didn't matter. All that mattered was to do something for God.

Another option—though somehow this sounded more dangerous than Africa—was going to seminary. But which seminary? Where would I get the money? And shouldn't I finish my college education first?

Only a week old in the faith and already paralyzed by indecision. Thankfully God didn't leave me floundering for long.

After the next church meeting I attended, the speaker invited those who wanted to be "baptized in the Holy Spirit" to meet in a separate room. I had never heard this phrase in my life. It sounded kind of strange, but I figured if I was going to be dodging wild animals in the Sahara, I had better get everything from God I could get.

I approached the man as soon as the meeting was over. "Sir," I asked, "what does it mean to be baptized in the Holy Spirit? I gave my life to Christ last week. Do I need this, this, uh, thing, this being baptized in the Holy Spirit?" Without a moment's hesitation he answered, "Going to that room and being filled with the Holy Spirit is the most important decision you will ever make as a Christian."

Meditate on 2 Corinthians 3:5-6. Are Christians competent (on their own) to do anything worthwhile for God?

(Since then, I've often wondered why he spoke so emphatically. Perhaps he saw in my eyes the look of a fanatic—someone who carefully considers all the options before flying off half-cocked. That was me.)

Nervously I entered the room and slid into a pew with twenty other folks who looked equally confused. I waited uneasily. Though I wanted all God had for me, this seemed very unusual. Eventually a young man came in and read some passages from the Bible. He explained what it meant to be baptized in the Spirit. Then he and some others began praying for us.

What followed was the most glorious thing, next to becoming a Christian, that has ever happened to me. I look back now and realize that my decision to seek this experience with the Holy Spirit was...well, the most important decision I have ever made as a Christian.

---

1 Other than your response to the gospel, what is the single biggest decision you have made in your life?

Who Is the Holy Spirit?

Theologian Gordon Fee writes of a seminary student who once confessed, "God the Father makes perfectly good sense to me; and God the Son I can quite understand; but the Holy Spirit is a gray, oblong blur."[1] Since most Christians have felt that way at one time or another, let's start with a foundational (but not simple) question: Who is the Holy Spirit?

Scripture speaks of God the Father, the Son, and the Holy Spirit—one God in three persons, commonly known as the Trinity. They are the same in essence, equal, and eternal. The Father is not the Son and the Son is not the Holy Spirit, yet each is truly deity.

For Further Study:
For an especially clear reference to the Trinity, see Matthew 28:19.

The Bible refers to this third person of the Trinity in a number of ways: the Spirit (John 3:6-8), the Holy Spirit (Luke 11:13), the Spirit of God (1 Corinthians 3:16), the Spirit of the Lord (Luke 4:18), the Spirit of Jesus (Acts 16:6-7), the Spirit of his Son (Galatians 4:6), and the Counselor (John 16:7), to name a few. Scripture also reveals many of the Holy Spirit's personal qualities. He has a mind (Romans 8:27), possesses knowledge (1 Corinthians 2:11), teaches (John 14:26), speaks (John 16:13), guides (John 16:13), and experiences grief (Ephesians 4:30), among other things. The Spirit's role is distinct from that of the Father or the Son. We'll look at his specific functions in the next section, but one Bible teacher summed them up well by describing the Spirit as "the Resident Agent of God in the Church and the earth."[3]

> **❝** In dealing with the Spirit, we are dealing with none other than the personal presence of God himself.[2] **❞**
> —Gordon Fee

The Holy Spirit isn't an "it." He isn't merely the *power* of God or the *influence* of God. He *is* God. And I think you'll be amazed to learn what a pivotal role he plays in your life as a Christian.

Ten Things the Spirit Does for You

1. The Spirit causes you to be born again. As we saw in the first study of this book, your salvation was initiated by God. And it was specifically carried out through the ministry of the Holy Spirit. Listen to what Jesus told the Jewish ruler Nicodemus: "I tell you the truth, no one can enter the kingdom of God unless he is born of water and the Spirit. Flesh gives birth to flesh, but *the Spirit gives birth to spirit*" (John 3:5-6). Paul also speaks of the Holy Spirit's role in regeneration: "He saved us through the washing of rebirth and renewal *by the Holy Spirit*, whom he poured out on us generously through Jesus Christ our Savior" (Titus 3:5-6).

2. The Spirit convicts you of sin. "When he comes," Jesus said of the Spirit, "he will convict the world of guilt in regard to sin and righteousness and judgment" (John 16:8). You undoubtedly know what that conviction feels like. Maybe you've experienced it as a sharp inward jab, or perhaps a dull spiritual ache. The Spirit was showing you that in some area you had violated God's will for your life, and it didn't feel very good at all.

Meditate on Revelation 3:19. How does God treat those he loves?

The Holy Spirit works in concert with God's Word to convict you when you sin. First, God's Word informs your mind of his standards. When you depart from those standards, the Spirit uses the Word to prick your conscience. It hurts, but conviction is a merciful gift from God. If the Spirit didn't convict us of sin, we would never obtain the freedom that comes through repentance.

3. The Spirit helps you put sin to death. Once he exposes sin in your life, the Spirit comes alongside to help you overcome it. No area of his ministry is more critical: "For if you live according to the sinful nature, you will die; but if by the Spirit you put to death the misdeeds of the body, you will live" (Romans 8:13).

The Spirit seeks to glorify God by conforming you to the image of his Son. You may have already experienced "Holy Spirit housecleaning" in your speech, actions, desires, thoughts, or motives. But as Romans 8:13 shows, God won't scrub sin from your life while you sleep. You are responsible to fight sin—not flirt with it, tolerate it, or yield to it. With the help of the Holy Spirit you are to put sin to death by saying "no" to the wayward appetites of your flesh and "yes" to the righteous commands of God's Word.

Don't try putting sin to death by yourself. You can't do it. You must have the Spirit's help. By responding to his conviction and receiving his strength on a daily basis, you can overpower the sin that tries to overpower you. And in the place of those

> To walk in the Spirit and be led by the Spirit then means something more than miracles. It means victory over the desires and impulses of the flesh. It means crucifying those desires. It means cultivating the fruit of the Spirit, for the fruit of the Spirit is the best antidote to the lusts of the flesh.[4]
>
> —**Stanley Horton**

sinful habits that once controlled you, the Spirit will cultivate a wonderful crop of new fruit—his love, joy, peace, patience, kindness, goodness, faithfulness, gentleness, and self-control (Galatians 5:22-23).

4. The Spirit guides you. During my struggle to choose between African missions and seminary training, I was relieved to discover that God, through the work of the Holy Spirit, would guide me. Jesus promises such guidance very clearly in the Bible: "But when he, the Spirit of truth, comes, he will guide you into all truth. He will not speak on his own; he will speak only what he hears, and he will tell you what is yet to come" (John 16:13). Theologian J. Rodman Williams writes that when the new birth occurs, "The Holy Spirit lays claim upon a person… so as to be the controlling and guiding reality [in his or her life]. Henceforward one is to move under the direction of the Holy Spirit."[5]

For Further Study:
Read Galatians 5:25. What do you think it means to "keep in step with the Spirit"?

Following the Spirit's lead requires discernment. There are people who claim the Spirit led them to neglect their children, or led them to default on a loan, or led them to invest their tithes and offerings in a new Jeep Cherokee. But we can say confidently that none of these decisions were initiated by the Spirit. You see, the Spirit's leading is never arbitrary. The night before his death Jesus told his disciples the Spirit would guide them "into all truth." As he prayed for them later that night, he asked his Father, "Sanctify them by the truth; your word is truth" (John 17:17). Since God's Word is truth, and the Spirit guides us into all truth, the Spirit will never lead you to want, say, think, or do anything outside the boundaries of God's Word. His guidance will always be consistent with Scripture. This principle will help immensely as you seek to discern whether or not "a leading" is truly from God.

---

2 In which of the following situations would you sense a need for God's guidance?

❑ Deciding whether or not to attend college

❑ Deciding which checkout line to take at Wal-Mart

❑ Deciding whether or not to get married

❑ Deciding whether to accept a certain job offer

❑ Deciding whether to cook "Squid Supreme" for dinner

❑ Deciding whether or not to change your child's diaper

---

5. The Spirit teaches you spiritual things. Though God will regularly instruct you through others, he will also reveal things to you directly. The Holy Spirit "will teach you all things," Jesus assured his disciples, "and will remind you of everything I have said to you" (John 14:26).

For Further Study:
How would you sum up the remarkable promise made in 1 Corinthians 2:12-16?

A few weeks after I became a Christian, I was reading in the Gospel of Luke about Mary and her relative Elizabeth being pregnant. As I studied it, something began coming into focus. Could it be that Jesus and John the Baptist were...related? Possibly even cousins? I ran to share the news with one of my friends. I was so excited to have made a spiritual discovery!

Anyone could have discovered the same with a little bit of study. What was memorable about this event, though, is how the Holy Spirit unfolded the passage's significance to me. Suddenly I had fresh insight about how Jesus must have felt when he heard John was beheaded. It was bad enough thinking about the severed head on a platter. But John wasn't simply some wild prophet who had barked out warnings in the desert. He was family. It must have affected Jesus deeply to know that the first person to die for his sake was a relative, someone he had probably eaten with and played with while growing up.

The Spirit has probably taught you things much more significant than this—things about yourself, about the character of God, or about your Christian life. It is his role to illuminate the Word of God. Unless he opens your ears and eyes, you cannot fully understand or benefit from Scripture. Make it a habit to ask the Holy Spirit for understanding and insight every time you read your Bible or listen to the Word being preached.

6. The Spirit helps you worship. When you were born again, the Spirit himself planted deep in your heart a desire to worship the Lord. In fact, worship is one of the chief purposes for your existence: "But you are a chosen people, a royal priesthood, a holy nation, a people belonging to God, that you may declare the praises of him who called you out of darkness into his wonderful light" (1 Peter 2:9).

> **❝** Worship is one's heart expression of love, adoration, and praise to God with an attitude and acknowledgment of his supremacy and Lordship...It is the unashamed pouring out of our inner self upon the Lord Jesus Christ in affectionate devotion.[6] **❞**
> —Bob Sorge

A heart touched by the Spirit won't be able to confine worship to a Sunday meeting. Every day you are to offer God sacrifices of thanks and praise, inspired and enabled

Meditate on Romans 8:15-16. Only by the Spirit can we intimately worship the Father.

by the Spirit of God. This is no lifeless obligation. The person who has been genuinely born again and filled with the Spirit will experience a deep desire and need to express affection for God through worship.

7. The Spirit helps you pray. "We do not know how to pray as we should," wrote the apostle Paul, "but the Spirit Himself intercedes for us with groanings too deep for words" (Romans 8:26 NAS). The Holy Spirit will teach you how to pray with your *native* tongue—that is, normal words expressing the burdens of your heart. He will also enable you to pray with a *new* tongue. Christians are able to speak in other tongues once they have been baptized in the Spirit. (We'll discuss this more at the end of the study.) Finally, the Holy Spirit may lead you to pray with *no* tongue at all. Paul carried burdens so heavy, so grievous that words couldn't express them. But through the Spirit, he poured out his heart before God with sighs and groanings.[7]

> **❝** If we have ears to hear, hearts to receive, and wills to obey, we may trust ourselves to our Heavenly Teacher to lead us into this deep mystery of prayer.[8] **❞**
>
> —**Arthur Wallis**

A friend of mine was on a golf trip with several other pastors when he received an urgent message from the clubhouse. His wife, who was a couple of months pregnant, had developed complications. It seemed almost certain she would miscarry. During the long drive home he prayed intensely, first in his own words and then in the Spirit. As he did so, his faith and hope increased. Today he has a beautiful daughter to remind him that the Spirit's prayers in us and for us are mighty indeed.

8. The Spirit imparts supernatural gifts that equip you for service. "The Little Drummer Boy" was my favorite Christmas carol when I was a kid. Do you remember the words? They describe a poor little boy who wanted to give something to his King, yet had nothing of value—no gold or frankincense or myrrh. All he had was the tattered drum slung around his neck. Then, with a heart of delight, he realized what he had to offer was a song. He could play his drum for the King!

This simple song points to an important biblical truth. None of us has anything of value to give our King. He doesn't need our money. He doesn't need our things. The fact is, he doesn't "need" anything. But he does desire. He desires that his children willingly live for his glory. And through the Spirit Jesus has given each of us spiritual gifts with which to glorify him.

47

For Further Study:
Read Hebrews 2:3-4.
To what do the gifts of
the Holy Spirit testify?

Scripture says, "When he ascended on high, he led captives in his train and gave gifts to men" (Ephesians 4:8). The New Testament lists these spiritual gifts in several places (see, for example, Romans 12, 1 Corinthians 12, and Ephesians 4). Among them are gifts such as healing, mercy and faith. Some Christians serve the church with gifts of teaching or prophecy or exceptional generosity. I don't have space here to discuss spiritual gifts in detail, but I have recommended several books at the end of this study that do. Take advantage of them!

---

3 Most of the spiritual gifts mentioned in the New Testament are listed below. If you think God may have given you one of these gifts, put a ✔ beside it. Circle any gifts you would like to receive from God.

- ☐ Teaching (Ro 12:7)
- ☑ Serving (Ro 12:7)
- ☐ Encouraging (Ro 12:8)
- ☐ Giving (Ro 12:8)
- ☑ Leadership (Ro 12:8)
- ☐ Mercy (Ro 12:8)
- ☐ Faith (1Co 12:9)
- ☐ Healing (1Co 12:9)
- ☐ Prophecy (1Co 12:10)
- ☐ Tongues (1Co 12:10)
- ☐ Administration (1Co 12:28)
- ☐ Helps (1Co 12:28)
- ☑ Word of wisdom (1Co 12:8)
- ☐ Miracles (1Co 12:28)
- ☑ Word of knowledge (1Co 12:8)
- ☐ Discernment (1Co 12:10)

(Ro = Book of Romans; 1Co = 1st Corinthians; 1Ti = 1st Timothy)

---

9. The Spirit empowers you to witness. When the Holy Spirit takes up residence in you, your life *becomes* a witness. The changes he makes in you give evidence of the fact that God is alive and powerful. But when you are baptized in the Spirit, you also receive power to *be* a witness. You find welling up from within a boldness to share your faith with others. How else could the same disciples who abandoned Jesus before his crucifixion speak out forcefully in his name at Pentecost? Their Lord had already foreseen it: "But you will receive *power* when the Holy Spirit comes on you; and you will be my witnesses…" (Acts 1:8).

I needed that power on a recent flight to Cleveland. As I took my seat by the aisle, I sensed the Holy Spirit wanted me to talk with the two ladies beside me. In fact, before I could even get my seat belt buckled, the lady in the center asked, "Are you a preacher?" That was all the confirmation I needed.

For Further Study:
Compare the cowardice of Peter in Luke 22:54-62 with his courage in Acts 2:14-41. The Spirit made all the difference!

The ladies were traveling to a psychology conference in Canada. As we spoke frankly about child-raising, motives for living, and other sensitive issues, two things became evident. First, these ladies were strongly opposed to a biblical worldview. They weren't interested in polite discussion—they wanted to roast me. Second, these two weren't the only ones listening. It seemed like everyone around us was tuning in as I used Scripture to discuss the benefits of spanking and the dangers of "self-esteem."

The lady by the window made little effort to mask her disdain at what I was saying. Finally she rolled over and went to sleep. But after a few moments of silence the lady beside me said, "You know, it wasn't a coincidence you sat here. I needed to hear some of these things."

Did she throw herself down in the aisle and cry out for God's forgiveness? No—but it appeared she had moved a few steps closer to receiving Christ. And her friend, while outwardly unchanged, had at least heard the truth.

How did this happen? I deserve no credit. The Holy Spirit motivated me to witness—and gave me boldness to declare God's truth in a rather intimidating setting.

10. The Spirit counsels and helps you. Imagine the disciples' sorrow as the truth sank in: their Master was leaving. Not only would he be crucified, but he would soon return to his Father in heaven. Yet after announcing this, Jesus quickly assured them he would not leave them alone: "I will ask the Father, and he will give you another Counselor to be with you forever—the Spirit of truth. The world cannot accept him, because it neither sees him nor knows him. But you know him, for he lives with you and will be in you" (John 14:16-17).

> **❝** The Holy Spirit is intended to be real, powerful, and lovingly intimate in Christians' lives. He becomes just as much to us as if we actually possessed the personal companionship of Jesus of Nazareth, walking and talking with us along the way, and pervading our lives with His Presence.[9] **❞**
> —**Donald Gee**

What did Jesus mean when he called the Holy Spirit the "Counselor"? The word in Greek is *parakletos*. According to theologian Stanley Horton, it speaks of "one called to help, aid, advise, or counsel someone."[10]

The Spirit was no second-string substitute. "I tell you the truth," said Jesus, *"it is for your good that I am going away.* Unless I go away, the Counselor will not come to you; but if I go, I will send him to you" (John 16:7). Think about it. As exciting as it would have been to walk and talk with our Lord in the flesh, it's actually better to walk with his Spirit, the Parakletos, who counsels us, helps us, and lives in us.

Drawing Closer to the Spirit

I trust by now we've gotten past the "gray, oblong blur" stage in our understanding of the Holy Spirit. We've seen that he is God. We've looked at ten of the ways he ministers in, to, and through the Christian. That leaves us with at least one more critical question: How does one relate to the Holy Spirit? How can you insure that he is living and working in you?

Meditate on Romans 8:9-11. Do you see the benefits of having God's Spirit living in you?

Those outside of Christ cannot relate to the Spirit of God. If you have been born again, however, be assured that the Spirit is already at work in you. Jesus said it this way: "The world cannot accept him [the Spirit], because it neither sees him nor knows him. *But you know him*, for he lives with you and will be in you" (John 14:17). The moment you were born again the Spirit came to dwell in you. That's why Paul could encourage Timothy, "Guard the good deposit that was entrusted to you—guard it with the help of the Holy Spirit who *lives in us*" (2 Timothy 1:14).

Scripture makes a distinction between being *indwelt* by the Spirit (which happens when you are born again) and being *baptized* in the Holy Spirit (which can occur either when you are born again or some time later). The term baptism is significant. "It depicts vividly the idea of being enveloped in the reality of the Holy Spirit," writes Dr. J. Rodman Williams. "Since to be baptized in water means literally to be immersed in, plunged under, and even drenched or soaked with, then to be baptized in the Holy Spirit can mean no less than that."[11] Being baptized in the Spirit is a distinct event through which the believer gains an increased awareness of God's presence and ability to exercise the powers of the age to come. Few ever forget this encounter.

(If you're not sure whether you've been baptized in the Spirit, then the chances are good that you have not been.

> ❝ The Spirit promised by the Father, sent forth by the Son, surrounds, encloses, immerses those to whom He comes. Nothing is left untouched or unaffected. It is as if one were bathed in the reality of God.[12] ❞
> —**J. Rodman Williams**

What a wonderful experience awaits you! We'll talk about that more in the next section.)

It is the Spirit's work to baptize you into Christ (the new birth), but Christ's work to baptize you in the Spirit. Though we are baptized in the Spirit just once, the Bible shows the importance of being filled again (and again and again) with the Spirit. Peter, for example, was filled twice soon after his initial experience at Pentecost (see Acts 4:8 and 4:31). The late Arthur Wallis wrote,

For Further Study: For examples of the disciples being filled afresh with the Spirit after their initial experience at Pentecost, see Acts 4:8 and 4:31.

> We don't need to be baptized in water every week, nor do we need a weekly baptism in the Spirit. But the first experience does need renewing or recharging, which is usually called being filled or anointed. There are many fillings or anointings, but only one baptism.[13]

When asked why he repeatedly petitioned the Lord to fill him with his Spirit, evangelist D.L. Moody responded, "Because I leak!" Don't we all?

---

4 Pop Quiz! To make sure you have understood this potentially confusing topic, circle "T" or "F" for each of the following statements.

(Answers printed upside down at bottom of page.)

	True	False
☐ The Holy Spirit dwells in all who are born again	T	F
☐ Even non-Christians have God's Spirit in them	T	F
☐ Being "indwelt by the Spirit" and "baptized in the Spirit" refer to the same experience	T	F
☐ You can be born again without being baptized in the Spirit	T	F
☐ Christians can be filled repeatedly with the Spirit	T	F

How Can I Be Baptized in the Holy Spirit?

The invitation Jesus shouted out in the crowded streets of Jerusalem still stands today: "'If anyone is thirsty, let him come to me and drink. Whoever believes in me, as the

Answers: T, F, F, T, T

51

Scripture has said, streams of living water will flow from within him.' By this he meant the Spirit, whom those who believed in him were later to receive" (John 7:37-39).

If you desire more of God's Spirit, this passage shows that three things are necessary. I'm indebted to Arthur Wallis for the following concise summary:

Thirst—a deep longing for God to meet you in this way. God creates thirst and satisfies it. If you're not thirsty, ask God why. If you have been filled, thirst for more.

Come—to Jesus, who baptizes in the Spirit, and ask. God gives to those who ask (Luke 11:13). But more than asking is needed.

Drink—that means to lay hold of the blessing by faith. Jesus says, "Whatever you ask for in prayer, believe that you have received it [that's when you start drinking], and it will be yours" (Mark 11:24). Drinking is an act of faith.[14]

As you pursue baptism in the Spirit, get advice from a mature Christian with proven character who has had this experience. Several times in the Book of Acts, believers were baptized in the Spirit when others laid hands on them and prayed (Acts 8:17, 9:17, 19:6). Don't underestimate the power of this simple act.

> **"** Our greatest danger, I feel today, is to quench the Spirit. This is no age to advocate restraint; the church today does not need to be restrained, but to be aroused, to be awakened, to be filled with a Spirit of glory.[15] **"**
>
> —**D. Martyn Lloyd-Jones**

"Speaking in tongues" is one common indicator that someone has been baptized in the Holy Spirit. This is a phenomenon in which the Spirit supernaturally enables a believer to speak in a heavenly or earthly language previously unknown and unlearned. Because tongues are misunderstood by many today, let's briefly discuss this particular spiritual gift.

Speaking in tongues was a prevalent feature of church life in the first century. Paul himself told the Corinthians, "I thank my God that I speak in tongues more than all of you" (1 Corinthians 14:18). He highlighted three benefits of this practice that should stimulate your interest:

■ "For anyone who speaks in a tongue does not speak to men but to God" (1 Corinthians 14:2). Though unintelligible to you and others, tongues express praise and thanksgiving to God (1 Corinthians 14:16-17) and declare "the wonders of God" (Acts 2:11).

> **"** We should make a deliberate effort at the outset of every day to recognize the person of the Holy Spirit...We should continue to walk throughout the day in a relationship of communication and communion with the Spirit mediated through our knowledge of the word, relying upon every office of the Holy Spirit's role...mentioned in Scripture.[16] **"**
>
> **—Richard Lovelace**

■ "Indeed, no one understands him; he utters mysteries with his spirit" (1 Corinthians 14:2). When you don't know exactly how to articulate what is on your heart, speaking in tongues enables your spirit to commune directly with God.

■ "He who speaks in a tongue edifies himself" (1 Corinthians 14:4). As the church at Corinth proved, this can easily get out of control. But who doesn't need edifying from time to time? When you exercise the gift of speaking in tongues, you will receive fresh strength and hope in your inner man. One can be baptized in the Spirit without receiving tongues, but it is a gift well worth pursuing.

As we bring this section to a close, I'm painfully aware that I may have raised more questions than I answered. "There are few subjects harder to present from a highly doctrinal standpoint than the subject of the Holy Spirit," notes pastor Dick Iverson. I fully agree—especially in a study this brief.

For Further Study: To see the main purpose of tongues and all other spiritual gifts, read 1 Corinthians 14:26.

I will be satisfied if these pages have made you a little more thirsty for the Spirit. And I encourage you to read the books recommended on the next page. They go into much greater depth explaining the work and person of the Holy Spirit. I have no doubt they will persuade you even more of this study's main point: Being baptized in the Holy Spirit may be the most important decision you will ever make as a Christian. ■

GROUP DISCUSSION 1. What kinds of life circumstances could make a person "thirsty" for the Spirit's presence and power?

2. Without looking, can you recall five things the Spirit does for us?

3. Are you currently facing a decision or situation in which you need God's guidance?

4. Identify one specific thing the Holy Spirit has taught you.

5. What do you think it means to "live by the Spirit" (Galatians 5:25)?

6. How did you answer Question 3 about spiritual gifts on page 48?

7. Why should you be *baptized* in the Holy Spirit if he already dwells in you?

8. Do you have any other questions or comments about this study?

RECOMMENDED READING *Surprised by the Power of the Spirit* by Jack Deere (Grand Rapids, MI: Zondervan Publishing House, 1993)

Joy Unspeakable by D. Martyn Lloyd-Jones (Wheaton, IL: Harold Shaw Publishers, 1984)

What the Bible Says About the Holy Spirit by Stanley Horton (Springfield, MO: Gospel Publishing House, 1976)

Answer to Warm-Up
(from page 41): As of 1995, the average citizen of **Mexico** drank 333 eight-ounce servings of Coca-Cola products each year. The U.S. came next (310 servings), followed by Australia (274), Norway (256), Israel (222), Zimbabwe (62), Russia (5), and China (3). If the Holy Spirit could be measured in 8-oz. servings, do you think Christians around the world would drink as much of the Spirit as they drink Coke? (Source: Coca-Cola, Office of Industry and Consumer Affairs, Atlanta, GA)

SOME THINGS TO KNOW ABOUT YOURSELF

BIBLE STUDY 2 Corinthians 5:16-21

WARM-UP If you research the family backgrounds of U.S. presidents, some appear to have been born for greatness, while others seemed destined for obscurity. Judging purely by family roots, how would you have expected these men to turn out?

	Greatness	Obscurity
George Washington	❑	❑
Thomas Jefferson	❑	❑
Andrew Jackson	❑	❑
Abraham Lincoln	❑	❑
Theodore Roosevelt	❑	❑
John F. Kennedy	❑	❑
Ronald Reagan	❑	❑

(See page 68 for answers)

PERSONAL STUDY What does it mean to become a Christian? What *really* happened the day you submitted your life to God? Most likely it went something like this:

You heard about Jesus from a friend or family member, or perhaps at a church service. As God's Word did its work, you sensed the convicting activity of the Holy Spirit in your heart (though you didn't know to call it that). You probably became very aware of your own sins. Then, while the sting of conviction was still fresh, someone explained that Jesus died on the Cross for you—an act of infinite love which made it possible for you to be reconciled to God. Drawn by God's merciful initiative, you responded to the gospel by confessing your sinfulness and accepting

55

Christ by faith as your Lord and Savior. Maybe you were given a Bible to commemorate the event, and you went home bursting with new excitement about life...and a thousand unanswered questions.

But is this all that happened?

Out with the Old, In with the New

Having your sin forgiven is just one of the blessings you received when God saved you. Don't misunderstand—I would never want to minimize the significance of this act. Every Christian should be overwhelmed to realize that the condemning sin which once hung over us now hangs nailed permanently to the Cross (Colossians 2:13-15). But as amazing as forgiveness is, it is only the beginning of your inheritance in Christ. Something absolutely fantastic has occurred! The Bible describes it this way:

> Therefore, if anyone is in Christ, he is a *new creation*; the old has gone, the new has come! (2 Corinthians 5:17)

The day you became a Christian, you became a completely different person. "A Christian is a radically changed person the moment he or she trusts Christ," writes Jerry Bridges. "This doesn't mean we become 'saints' in practice overnight. It does mean a new creation —a new principle of life— has been planted within us by the Holy Spirit, and we can never be the same again."[2]

Your change from an "old creation" to a "new creation" was dramatic and irreversible. You aren't simply a spruced-up version of what you were before. Unlike the cars that roll off the assembly lines in Detroit every year, you have more than a new paint job and aerodynamic design to distinguish you from last year's model. There's a totally new engine under the hood! And even that illustration falls pitifully short of describing what has taken place. You have been transformed from one being to another.

> **❝** A Christian is not simply a person who gets forgiveness, who gets to go to heaven, who gets the Holy Spirit, who gets a new nature. Mark this—*a Christian is a person who has become someone he was not before.* A Christian, in terms of his deepest identity, is a SAINT, a born child of God, a divine masterpiece, a child of light, a citizen of heaven...Becoming a Christian is not just getting something, no matter how wonderful that something may be. *It is becoming someone.*[1] **❞**
>
> —**David C. Needham**

For Further Study:
Just how bad was the "old creation" that has been replaced? Romans 3:9-18 spells it out in frightening detail.

I doubt you saw all these changes when you looked at yourself in the bathroom mirror this morning. But God's Word is true. In the following sections we will explore three things that have changed about you now that you are a new creation in Christ.

---

1 Compare a monarch butterfly to the caterpillar it once was, and it's easy to see something has changed. Can you detect any evidence showing how you as a "new creation" are different from who you were before? Jot down your thoughts.

Your Spiritual Condition Has Changed

Before you were born again, God saw you as dead, dark and doomed. You were *dead* in sin, unresponsive to spiritual things and incapable of any spiritual life apart from God's help (Colossians 2:13; Ephesians 2:1). Your heart was *dark*, unable to understand God or obey his commands (Ephesians 4:17-19). As a result, you were *doomed* to bear the full guilt of your sins and pay the horrific but just penalty for them (Matthew 10:28; Romans 6:23).

Your spiritual condition changed the moment you were born again. The spiritually alive (Holy Spirit) touched the spiritually dead (you) and brought you to life. God enlightened your dark heart so that you could see and pursue him. He changed it from a heart of stone into a heart of flesh (Ezekiel 36:26). Finally, God canceled your death sentence by nailing it to the Cross (Colossians 2:14). No longer are you sitting on Death Row, awaiting torment in hell. Instead, you have the incredible guarantee that you will be resurrected from the dead and spend eternity with God in heaven.

Your Standing Before God Has Changed

The Bible says you were once God's enemy. Did you know that? You weren't just apathetic or passive toward him. You weren't just a cynic or an agnostic. You were

Meditate on Colossians 1:21-23.
Isn't it hard to believe God would treat his former enemies with such mercy?

actively opposed to his rule and reign in your life (Romans 8:7). And he was opposed to you. But your standing before God changed completely the day you became a Christian.

■ Once you were God's enemy; now you're his friend.

■ Once you were at war with him (what a mismatch!)— now you have peace with God through your Lord Jesus Christ (Romans 5:1).

■ You were guilty of great sin; now you are justified by Christ and free from condemnation (Romans 8:1).

■ You used to be cut off from God and without hope in this world; now he will never leave you or forsake you (Hebrews 13:5).

■ Once you were far away from him, but now you "have been brought near through the blood of Christ" (Ephesians 2:13).

■ Once you faced the inescapable wrath of your heavenly Judge; today you know the love and provision of your heavenly Father. He even invites you to approach his throne boldly with your requests so that he can give grace and help in your time of need (Hebrews 4:16). Praise be to God for his wonderful work on our behalf!

Your Identity Has Changed

Prior to regeneration, you thought of yourself primarily in terms of your own traits and accomplishments. Maybe you took pride in your musical talent or athletic ability. Perhaps your life revolved around education, career advancement, or financial status. It could be that you were absorbed in your physical appearance or winsome personality. Whatever the case, one thing is clear: Your sense of well-being depended on *you*. You were the center of your universe.

This explains why so many people today are plagued by neurosis. Once their money dries up or their hair falls out; when they gain a pound or when the fingers fumble over the keyboard; when their Harvard degree no longer impresses the company president, they encounter a major identity

> 44 Because of Christ's death in our place, God's justice is now completely satisfied. God can now, without violating His justice or His moral law, forgive us freely, completely, and absolutely.[3] 77
>
> —Jerry Bridges

Meditate on Philippians 2:1. Are you encouraged to know you are united with Christ?

crisis. Why? Because they measure their worth on the basis of external or material criteria. And sooner or later they are bound to come up short.

But now that you are a Christian, you have been united with Christ, and that changes the reference point of your identity. When the Spirit of Jesus entered your heart, you experienced a living merger with him. A metamorphosis has occurred! You have been joined with God himself.

Scripture uses two phrases interchangeably to describe this union. In some passages it says we are "in Christ," or "in him." In other places it says Christ is "in us." There is at least one verse that combines both of these: "We know that we live *in him* and he *in us*, because he has given us of his Spirit" (1 John 4:13). Either way, the amazing fact is that you have been united with Christ.

---

2 Listed below are a few of the riches that make up our inheritance in Christ. Put a ✔ beside any for which you are especially thankful.

❏ Forgiveness of sin   ❏ Eternal life

❏ Justification   ❏ Adoption by God

❏ The Holy Spirit   ❏ Power to change

❏ Gifts of the Spirit   ❏ Fullness in Christ

❏ Knowledge of truth   ❏ A purpose in life

❏ Peace with God   ❏ Faith

❏ Healing   ❏ Authority over demons

❏ Wisdom   ❏ _____

Introducing the New You!

Rather than maintaining a self-image based solely on your abilities or accomplishments, it's time to start seeing yourself as the person you now are in Christ.

A child of God. If this statement weren't so clearly affirmed in the Bible, it would be very difficult to believe. What father would kill his own (and only) beloved son in order to adopt a pack of renegade orphans? The idea is preposterous. And yet this is exactly what God did in order to make you part of his family:

For Further Study:
According to Ephesians 1:5 (New International Version), what two things motivated God to adopt you?

For you did not receive a spirit that makes you a slave again to fear, but you received the Spirit of sonship. And by him we cry, "Abba, Father." The Spirit himself testifies with our spirit that we are God's children. Now if we are children, then we are heirs—heirs of God and co-heirs with Christ, if indeed we share in his sufferings that we may also share in his glory. (Romans 8:15-17)

You don't deserve to be God's slave, much less his son or daughter. Nobody does. Yet he adopted you as his own. And as if that weren't enough, he made you a full heir to his infinite riches. "How great is the love the Father has lavished on us," wrote the apostle John, "that we should be called children of God! And that is what we are!" (1 John 3:1). Now he is your Father, you are his child, and you will relate to him this way for the rest of eternity.

A purchased possession. Some dear friends of mine have adopted children. It has cost them thousands of dollars, though their love for children made it seem like a small price. Your adoption into the family of God was costly, too. In order for you to be reconciled to your holy Father, someone had to pay for your sins.

That's why Jesus died. It wasn't for *his* sins that he hung on the Cross. Rather, he hung there despised by men and rejected by God because of *your* sins. He took your place. The sinless Lamb of God became sin for you in order that you might be spared God's judgment. The innocent One received the full blow of God's holy wrath on himself so you wouldn't have to experience

> **Lord Jesus, you are my righteousness, I am your sin. You took on you what was mine; you set on me what was yours. You became what you were not that I might become what I was not.**[4]
>
> —**Martin Luther**

it. That's why the Bible says, "You are not your own; you were bought at a price" (1 Corinthians 6:19-20). By shedding his precious blood, Jesus did more than forgive your sins—he purchased you. He owns you. You are his.

A follower of Jesus Christ. "If anyone would come after me," Jesus announced to the crowds, "he must deny himself and take up his cross daily and follow me" (Luke 9:23). The requirements haven't changed in the last two thousand years. Now that you are born again, you are to follow Jesus for the rest of your life.

Those who expect to have their sins forgiven and then go on their merry, self-centered way have obviously never studied their Bibles. As 1 John 2:6 says, "Whoever claims to live in him must walk as Jesus did." That means whenever there is a conflict between your desires and God's desires, you follow his path. As you might guess, this won't be easy. You will have to deny yourself certain pleasures. You will have to crucify certain desires. You will have to replace old sinful habits with new habits that please God. And yet the joy of following your Lord will more than compensate for any apparent loss.

Ambassadors of Christ's kingdom. One of the most distinguished streets in Washington, D.C. is Massachusetts Avenue. It is lined with embassies representing countries from all over the world. The ambassadors who live here, though residents of the United States, are chiefly concerned for their own countries. They are not interested in our crime problems or educational system or economy, except to the degree these issues influence the nation they serve. They are living in one country but living *for* another.

Meditate on 2 Corinthians 5:15. Since Christ died for us, shouldn't we be eager to live for him?

So are you! When you became a Christian, your citizenship switched from earth to heaven (Philippians 3:20). "We are therefore Christ's ambassadors," says Paul, "as though God were making his appeal through us" (2 Corinthians 5:20). Your allegiance has changed. You aren't living for yourself or this world's values any more—you represent the Lord Jesus Christ and his kingdom. He calls you to be a faithful emissary of your new "country" and its values. As Christ's ambassador you are to live in a way which testifies that Jesus is Ruler and Savior of the world.

Pursuing His Purpose

As you now see, you aren't the same person you were before God saved you. Your condition has changed, your standing with God has changed, and your identity has changed. But there's something else dramatically different about you: your purpose in life has changed as well.

The Lord didn't cross your path momentarily and say, "Excuse me...I know you are living for yourself, but you have a bunch of sin that needs to be forgiven. If you will just say this little prayer, I'll forgive your sins, then you can be on your independent, selfish way." No—salvation isn't some clip-on accessory. When God claimed you for himself, he fundamentally changed your purpose for living. Here are his two broad-brush objectives for your life.

Conformity to Christ. Though echoed throughout the New Testament, God's goal of making you like his Son is expressed especially well in Romans 8:28-29:

> And we know that in all things God works for the good of those who love him, who have been called according to his purpose. For those God foreknew he also predestined to be conformed to the likeness of his Son, that he might be the firstborn among many brothers.

Like any good father, God won't let you spend your entire life in spiritual diapers. Instead, he will orchestrate situations that stretch your character, that force you to grow. If anger or impatience has characterized your life, he will expose it and help you replace it with forbearance and self-control. He will shine his spotlight on your pride and self-centeredness, then lead to follow the humble example of his Son. Where your life has been bound up by greed and material accumulation, the Lord will change the priorities of your heart so that you crave his kingdom and his righteousness.

> ❝ Truly, at the day of judgment we shall not be examined [by] what we have read, but what we have done; not how well we have spoken, but how virtuously we have lived.[5] ❞
>
> **—Thomas a Kempis**

Ephesians 5:1 exhorts us, "Be imitators of God...." The command implies a lot more than superficial or cosmetic imitation. You're not merely to mimic or act like God; you are to become like him.

> You were taught, with regard to your former way of life, to put off your old self, which is being corrupted by its deceitful desires; to be made new in the attitude of your minds; and to *put on the new self, created to be like God* in true righteousness and holiness. (Ephesians 4:22-24)

There's a name for this process of being conformed to the image of Christ. It's called *sanctification*, and it's guaranteed to keep you busy for the rest of your life. However, you will find several books recommended at the end of this study that can greatly accelerate the process.

Glorifying God. Before you were converted, you were the supreme object of your own affections and energies. You lived to fulfill your own agenda. But now all that has changed. As a Christian, your mission in life is to live for the glory of God. Everything you do should be evaluated

For Further Study: Are you intimidated by the thought of spending your entire life becoming more like Christ? Let Paul's words in Philippians 3:12-14 stir up your faith.

in the light of this priority. Your speech, morals, attitudes, finances, hobbies, relationships, TV viewing, work habits, tax returns, and every other area of life should be devoted to pleasing and honoring the God who redeemed you. As God's Spirit transforms you from within, you should find yourself in agreement with the psalmist who said, "Not to us, O Lord, not to us but to your name be the glory, because of your love and faithfulness" (Psalm 115:1).

---

3 Briefly describe one area of your life (only one!) that still needs to be conformed to the image of Christ.

"If I'm So New, What's This Old Stuff?"

You've probably figured this one out on your own by now, but let me mention it anyway: Even new creations in Christ are tempted to sin. In fact, your battle against sin has really just begun. "My life didn't become complicated until I became a Christian," says theologian R.C. Sproul.[6] How many of us can identify with his words!

At the risk of being long-winded, let me share a story that confirms Dr. Sproul's remark.

The night I became a new creation, I had a sense of indescribable gratitude to the Lord. I also felt waves of appreciation for the man whose preaching had illumined the path of salvation for me. I viewed him as a spiritual father, a role model to follow in the things of God. He was someone I could emulate. To him I was probably a nameless speck among a sea of 2,000 other faces. But to me, C.J. Mahaney was a spiritual giant, the first Christian I had ever wanted to be like.

Meditate on Jeremiah 17:9. When you think your motives are pure and your actions are godly, watch out!

My sense of indebtedness to C.J. was genuine and deep. My own arrogance, as it turned out, was deeper still.

I made that unpleasant discovery a few weeks after my conversion, the day I joined a group of my new Christian friends to play basketball at a local gym. Basketball had been my life since junior high school, and I had been attending college on a basketball scholarship. But for the first time ever, I was playing ball as a Christian. And all around me were new friends who were equally in love with God and eager to serve him.

I wound up on the same team with a man named Gary, and it is here the plot begins to thicken. You see, Gary was a very nice person. Gary was a pastor. Gary cared about the feelings of others and wanted everyone to participate, whether they stunk or not. All that stuff was fine, mind you, but just not on my team. My objective was to win, and save the friendship bit for afterwards.

We would have won the first game easily had it not been for Gary. He kept passing the ball to others even though they had no clue what to do with it. Meanwhile, I was coming to a slow boil. I was trying to act like a Christian, but inside I felt ready to explode.

With the game hanging in the balance, Gary decided to give Ed (not his real name) a chance to score. Ed was the guy who had matching shorts, matching t-shirt, matching socks, and matching sneakers. But Ed wouldn't have known the difference between a basketball and a bowling ball. Within ten seconds, the other team had stripped the ball away from Ed and scored the winning lay-up.

Gary went over to console Ed. "Good try," he said. I sat down on the gym floor and leaned against the wall, steaming mad. During the break I made two resolutions. The first was to keep the ball from Gary so he couldn't pass it to Ed. The second was to win this game decisively. I wanted everyone in that gym to realize I had nothing to do with our first loss. And I intended to show the other team what "in your face" really meant. No prisoners. No mercy. Just simple domination. And more than likely, blood.

As I stood at the foul line ready to begin the next game, I got my first glimpse of the man who would be guarding me. It was C.J....the man who had shown me the way to salvation. The man who had inspired me to give all for Jesus. The man for whom I had felt such profound gratitude and affection.

But all I felt at that moment was a desire to crush the opposing team.

To make a long story short, I played a one-man game. I brought the ball in-bounds every time. I never passed it, even when the other guys were wide open. None of them had the ruthless drive an athlete needs in order to win in this cruel world, so I spared them the trouble. One thing was sure: we were not going to lose.

Meditate on Philippians 2:3-4. Is this something you would do naturally apart from the Spirit's help?

C.J. guarded me as well as he could, but I had the experience and the height advantage. Before his team even touched the ball, I had scored nine straight baskets. Eventually I missed and the other team got a couple of points. But then I got the ball back again, and in minutes the score was 13-2. At that point my conscience began bothering me a little—a very little—so I passed the ball to a couple of my teammates. (Not Gary and not Ed.) They shot, I rebounded, and put the ball in the hoop. We had won the game, 15-4, before most of us even worked up a decent sweat.

I felt great. This was more like it. I had really shown these guys who was hot stuff.

> Christians tend to sin out of habit. It is our habit to look out for ourselves instead of others, to retaliate when injured in some way, and to indulge the appetites of our bodies. It is our habit to live for ourselves and not for God. When we become Christians, we do not drop all this overnight. In fact, we will spend the rest of our lives putting off these habits and putting on habits of holiness.[7]
>
> —**Jerry Bridges**

But something devastating happened on the way to the water fountain. C.J. came up with a smile on his face and stuck out his hand. "Great game!" he said. "That was impressive."

I could have died. The sudden contrast between his Christlike character and my own pride and selfishness made me physically ill. It would have been easier had someone taken a broomstick and whacked it deep into my gut. I didn't know what to say.

I left the gym after that game more broken than I had ever been in my life. With increasing pain I realized how I had put my interests and ego ahead of others. What could have driven me to show off at the expense of someone I cared for so deeply? I went home and sobbed.

For Further Study:
How does God feel toward those who are broken-hearted over their sin? (See Psalm 51:17)

Later, when I couldn't contain myself any longer, I called C.J.'s home. His wife answered and said he was at a speaking engagement and wouldn't be home until late. *Great,* I thought, *I'm dying inside and he's off serving God.* I told her it was a matter of life and death that I speak with him that night. That's honestly how I felt.

For the next four hours I flip-flopped between being disappointed with myself (which was actually just pride) and heartfelt brokenness. Finally, at 11:30 p.m., the phone rang. It was C.J.

"You don't know me," I began, "but I'm the fellow you guarded at Kennedy High School this afternoon."

"Oh, yeah—great game!"

(Here I was, an emotional amoeba, and he was still trying to compliment me. Stop it already!)

I tried not to fall apart as I confessed how selfish I had been, how ashamed I was for putting the game ahead of fellowship and concern for others, and most importantly, how ugly my pride and arrogance must have been to God. I asked him to forgive me for embarrassing him instead of honoring him in front of all his friends. He was gracious about it and quickly extended forgiveness. But I learned a lesson that day I will never forget.

---

4 With which character do you identify most?

❏ **Steve:** The self-centered, "win at all costs" hoopster

❏ **Gary:** The selfless pastor with a heart to serve

❏ **C.J.:** The forgiving mentor who overlooked an offense

❏ **Ed:** The player who dressed better than he dribbled

Creature from the Black Lagoon

I have shared this lengthy illustration to underscore a critical point. Beneath the surface of our regenerated lives lies a foul cesspool of selfish motives and evil desires. Theologians call this *indwelling sin*. We may not see it, others may not see it, but God sees it. And it's ugly.

> ❝ Here dwells our enemy; this is the fort, the citadel of this tyrant, where it maintains a rebellion against God all our days. Sometimes it hath more strength, and consequently more success; sometimes less...but it is always in rebellion whilst we live.[8] ❞
>
> —**John Owen**

Even though you have undergone a miraculous metamorphosis through the work of the Holy Spirit, indwelling sin remains. You will fight it for the rest of your life. Sinclair Ferguson has stated that "the power of indwelling sin is no less real in the believer than it is in the unbeliever."[9] Whether you've been a Christian 24 hours or 24 years, the potential for serious sin lurks in your heart.

The apostle Paul understood this cesspool of indwelling sin. Not only did he help point it out to others, but he saw it in himself. This man who authored much of the New

Testament, planted many churches, experienced countless hardships for the sake of Christ, and boldly proclaimed the gospel wherever he traveled continued to battle indwelling sin. Years after his conversion, and well into his ministry, he lamented over the wretchedness of his soul. Listen closely as he shares his inward struggle:

I do not understand what I do. For what I want to do I do not do, but what I hate I do. And if I do what I do not want to do, I agree that the law is good. As it is, it is no longer I myself who do it, but it is sin living in me. I know that nothing good lives in me, that is, in my sinful nature. For I have the desire to do what is good, but I cannot carry it out. For what I do is not the good I want to do; no, the evil I do not want to do—this I keep on doing. Now, if I do what I do not want to do, it is no longer I who do it, but it is sin living in me that does it.

So I find this law at work: When I want to do good, evil is right there with me. For in my inner being I delight in God's law; but I see another law at work in the members of my body, waging war against the law of my mind and making me a prisoner of the law of sin at work within my members. *What a wretched man I am!* Who will rescue me from this body of death? Thanks be to God, through Jesus Christ our Lord. (Romans 7:15-25)

> **“** Freedom from the dominion of sin is not...the same thing as freedom from its presence and influence...As an indwelling 'law,' or principle in our lives, it is in permanent readiness to act.[10] **”**
>
> —Sinclair Ferguson

What does all this mean? Simply that Paul had two opposing forces at work in him, battling for supremacy. Like him, you too will often experience a tug-of-war between the desire to do good and the desire to do evil. Sin lies hidden in your own heart, ready to jump out and ambush you when you least expect it. Grasp this and you will be helped immeasurably in your quest to grow as a Christian. But if you ignore this truth about indwelling sin, you will remain forever frustrated and confused about the battle which rages in your heart.

Meditate on Genesis 4:6-7. You'll have to stay on your toes if you hope to master sin.

At the moment he saved you, God delivered you from the wrath your sins deserved. He has united you with Christ and placed his Holy Spirit in you. He has made you a new creation. He has adopted you into his family and given you a new identity. He has purchased you for himself and made you his ambassador. He has given you a new heart. But until you die and go to heaven, you won't have a perfect one. Your bondage to sin has been broken, and yet the potential for sin, the pull of sin, and even the power of sin remain.

But it won't remain unchallenged. Like the valiant men and women who have served God in centuries past, you must arm yourself for battle against this indwelling foe. And in the strength of the Spirit, you must fight. ■

GROUP DISCUSSION

1. What would you do if you suddenly inherited a million dollars (tax free)?

2. Some people feel an immediate difference after being born again, and some don't. What was your experience?

3. What were the three "D's" of your spiritual condition before conversion? (See page 57)

4. Why must a Christian understand how bleak his or her spiritual condition was prior to regeneration?

5. What are some major things that have helped shape your identity?

6. Judging by your daily schedule, who owns your time and energy—you or God? Explain.

7. Describe one way in which you imitated God this week.

8. How long will it take the average Christian to outgrow sin? (This one is a little tricky.)

9. Do you have any remaining questions about this study?

Answers to Warm-Up (from page 55): In case you didn't know, **George Washington** and **Thomas Jefferson** grew up in wealthy Virginia families. **Andrew Jackson** was the son of poor Irish immigrants. **Abraham Lincoln** was born in a one-room log cabin. **Theodore Roosevelt** and **John F. Kennedy** came from New England families of high social standing. And **Ronald Reagan**, before rising to Hollywood stardom and the presidency, grew up as the son of a traveling shoe salesman. Praise God that our beginning doesn't have to determine our end!

RECOMMENDED READING

How Can I Change? by Robin Boisvert and C.J. Mahaney (Gaithersburg, MD: People of Destiny International, 1993)

Transforming Grace by Jerry Bridges (Colorado Springs, CO: NavPress, 1991)

Men Made New by John R.W. Stott (Grand Rapids, MI: Baker Book House, 1984)

SOME THINGS TO KNOW ABOUT YOUR BATTLE

BIBLE STUDY   Ephesians 6:10-18

WARM-UP   Which of the following are likely to be standard issue for U.S. Army soldiers by the year 2020?

❏ Wrist-mounted communicators

❏ Greatly improved night-vision glasses

❏ Pocket-size computers that process satellite data

❏ Computerized, laser-sighted rifles

❏ Electronic cloaking devices

(See page 85 for answer)

PERSONAL STUDY   I usually skim newspaper articles…but not this one. I was grimacing before I was halfway through. If there hadn't been a photograph with the article, I would have had a hard time believing it.

(I should warn you. The next few paragraphs are not for the squeamish. Read at your own discretion….)

On July 20, 1993, Donald "Butch" Wyman was cutting timber in a remote area 100 miles northeast of Pittsburgh. Suddenly the tree he was cutting fell on him, crushing his lower left leg and driving his foot into the ground. He was pinned. Moving the 30-inch thick trunk was impossible. And Butch was scared he would bleed to death if he waited for someone to find him.

He had only two options: either do the unthinkable, or die where he lay. Butch looked at his trapped leg one last time. Then, taking his pocket knife in hand, he cut his way through the mangled skin, muscle, nerves, and shattered bone of his leg. It only took 30 seconds, Butch told *USA Today*, "but even 30 seconds was too long."

Butch dragged himself up a hill to a nearby bulldozer, climbed in the cab, then drove to his truck and on to a nearby farmhouse. The photo accompanying the article showed Butch in a hospital bed, smiling and showing off his bandaged stump. Smiling? How could he be smiling? Because amputation was a lot better than death. As he told the reporter, "I have so much to live for that I did the only thing I could—chose life."[1]

I share this gruesome story for a reason. It tells the price one man had to pay to survive. Butch had no time to be passive or patient. If he ever hoped to see his family and friends again, he knew he had to act decisively. And so, when his own leg threatened to be the instrument of his death, he took radical action against it.

Living a victorious Christian life also requires radical action. You won't go to the extremes Butch Wyman did, but don't think you can take a laissez-faire approach to following Christ. You're in a battle. And your greatest enemy is within you.

Meditate on Matthew 5:29-30. Though Jesus knew sin could not be removed through self-mutilation, what do these statements reveal about his attitude toward sin?

The Battle Within

I've spoken with many Christians who were frustrated by this promise recorded in Romans 5:17: "Those who receive God's abundant provision of grace and the gift of righteousness [will] reign in life through the one man, Jesus Christ." Why does this passage bother them? Because they don't see any evidence they *are* reigning in life, especially in the areas where they are most vulnerable to temptation and sin.

The problem isn't with the promise. The problem stems primarily from their false expectations of the Christian life and a misunderstanding of sin.

> ❝ Sin is a state of heart, a condition of our inmost being. It is a state of corruption, of vileness, yes, even of filthiness in God's sight.[2] ❞
>
> —**Jerry Bridges**

Let's look briefly at what sin is and where it originates. Sin can be defined as "any failure to conform to the moral law of God in act, attitude, or nature."[3] It is more than a mere shortcoming or mistake or lapse in judgment. Sin is a violation of God's perfect moral standard. When we sin, we sin against him. "We never see sin aright," said W.S. Plumer, "until we see it as against God....All sin is against God in this sense: that it is his law that is broken, his authority that is despised, his government that is set at naught."[4] Sin always grieves God, often hurts others, and consistently boomerangs with personal consequences for the sinner.

So why *do* we sin? Having been justified (declared righteous) by a merciful God, why do we still find certain sins so appetizing, even though we know they are clearly off limits for a Christian?

Jesus pinpointed the nerve center of sin (a skill we need to learn) during a dialogue about hygiene. Some Pharisees had criticized the disciples for not washing their hands at mealtimes. Jesus used the occasion to make a powerful statement about indwelling sin:

For Further Study: According to Romans 5:12, how did sin enter the world? How widely did it spread?

> Don't you see that nothing that enters a man from the outside can make him "unclean"? For it doesn't go into his heart but into his stomach, and then out of his body…What comes out of a man is what makes him "unclean." For from within, out of men's hearts, come evil thoughts, sexual immorality, theft, murder, adultery, greed, malice, deceit, lewdness, envy, slander, arrogance and folly. All these evils come from inside and make a man "unclean." (Mark 7:18-23)

It would certainly be convenient if we could point to other people or outside circumstances as the cause of our sin. But Jesus' point is unavoidable: sin bubbles up out of the polluted cesspool of the human heart.

---

1 Which of the following do you feel has taken the greatest toll on our planet?

❑ The 1945 bombing of Hiroshima and Nagasaki

❑ The 1984 gas leak in Bhopal, India that killed 2,000

❑ The 1986 Chernobyl nuclear meltdown

❑ The 1989 Exxon Valdez oil spill (10 million gallons)

❑ Adam and Eve's sin and its continuing effects

The following illustration is geared more toward men, but I trust women will be able to relate. Imagine you have been limping around town for the last umpteen years in a run-down Ford Escort. It has 150,000 miles and isn't much to look at, but it gets you where you need to go. Then one Saturday morning, Gene—your neighbor and (former) friend—invites you over to see his brand new, loaded minivan. (As if he really needed one…he only has one kid!) You get in and are immediately overpowered by the new smell. Gripping the steering wheel, you fantasize you are flying down the highway with a worship tape cranked all the way up on his 15-speaker stereo (to give God the glory, of course). Then Gene throws your little dream trip into sudden reverse. "How's *your* bag of bolts holding up?" he asks with a smirk. "Got any floorboards left under all that rust?"

You smile politely and compliment Gene on his new van. Inside you are actively questioning the justice of God. On your way past your faithful Ford Escort, you mutter a few words you thought you'd forgotten and storm into the house, disgusted even to own such a piece of junk.

Now for the post-sin analysis…At first glance you may be tempted to think Gene caused your envy. Not only was he foolish enough to waste his money on a total luxury (in your opinion), but then he had the gall to invite you to sit in it so that you would have to act all excited for him. (At the very least, he could have rolled down the windows to get out that sickening new-car smell.)

> ❝ Scripture teaches that the *seat of sin* is to be found in the heart of man. 'Temptations and occasions put nothing into a man, but only draw out what was in him before.' All real sins proceed from the heart.[5] ❞
>
> **—Sinclair Ferguson**

But as we saw in Mark 7:18-23, Jesus doesn't start where we start. He wouldn't blame your envy on Gene's insensitivity or his new van. Instead, he would remind you that envy is dwelling within your heart, ready to jump out at the slightest provocation. This time it was Gene's van. Tomorrow it could just as easily be something else.

Someone once said the potential for the most heinous sin lies in the bosom of every man—Christians included. This is true because even after regeneration, the seeds of indwelling sin remain in our hearts. Listen to Sinclair Ferguson's insights on this subject:

What does Scripture mean by the heart? Sometimes it means the mind and the understanding, sometimes the will or the affections, sometimes the conscience, or the whole soul. Sin's strength in the heart lies in its unsearchable nature—there is always more there than can be discovered; it lies too in the deceitfulness of man's heart which is full of contradictions.[6]

Meditate on Isaiah 64:6. If this is what our righteous acts are like, how do you think our *sinful* acts appear to God?

Since we live with a heart that is inclined to stray from God's moral standards, how can we avoid grieving him? How can we cap this internal well that keeps spewing out sinful sludge? In past generations, some people squirreled away in monasteries and convents trying to escape the tempting influences of their day. One man, Simon Stylites, spent 36 years perched on a tiny platform sixty feet high thinking he could avoid sin by isolating himself from people and outward temptation. But neither he nor anyone else has found a way to escape the heart's magnetic attraction toward sin. Our most dangerous adversary, as the Puritan pastor John Owen recognized, is constantly attacking us from inside:

> There is an exceeding efficacy and power in the remainder of indwelling sin in believers with a constant inclination and working towards evil. Awake, therefore, all of you in whose hearts is any thing of the ways of God! Your enemy is not only *upon* you, as on Samson of old, but is *in* you also.[7]

Change Is Possible...but Not Overnight

Before anyone would have mistaken him for a saint, the renowned Augustine was a professional sinner. He spared himself no gutter: strong drink, sexual trysts, and all sorts of carnal pleasures were fair game. Then the Holy Spirit invaded his life and turned him into a radical follower of God. But not overnight. It is said that shortly after becoming a Christian, Augustine prayed, "Lord, give me chastity...just not yet!"

For Further Study: Read Hebrews 6:11-12. Can you find three qualities here that make change possible?

Like all of us, Saint Augustine faced the reality of indwelling sin. He knew he had to give up his sinful lifestyle, but within his heart there remained a craving for evil. He eventually changed, however, and began living a life pleasing to God. You are to do the same. In order to escape sin's enticing pull on your heart, however, you'll need a strategy—a three-part strategy.

Strategy #1: Avoid Temptation

Temptation strikes at the instant you begin drooling over Gene's new van. (Perhaps for you, ladies, it's Wendy's three-carat diamond engagement ring). The battle hinges on that moment of decision: Will you obey God or disobey? Will you yield to sin's enticement? Or will you subdue that

> **There is no man that is altogether free from temptations while he liveth on earth: for in ourselves is the root thereof, being born with an inclination to evil. When one temptation or tribulation goeth away, another cometh; and we shall ever have something to suffer.**[8]
>
> **—Thomas a Kempis**

desire and submit to God's will by rejoicing with Gene and Wendy?

Don't be surprised when you experience temptation. As Jesus told his disciples, "The spirit is willing, but the body is weak" (Matthew 26:41). Instead, you should find it comforting to know that your Lord himself was subjected to every possible outward temptation, yet never sinned (Hebrews 4:15). He can relate to your struggle. Better yet, he can help you *win* your struggle:

> No temptation has seized you except what is common to man. And God is faithful; he will not let you be tempted beyond what you can bear. But when you are tempted, he will also provide a way out so that you can stand up under it. (1 Corinthians 10:13)

So what's the secret? What is the escape route from anger, resentment, pride, lust, envy, fear, and the host of other sins that tempt us?

For Further Study:
What advice does Paul give in the following verses? (1 Corinthians 6:18, 10:14; 1 Timothy 6:11; 2 Timothy 2:22)

The first and best strategy is to avoid, wherever possible, those situations that might entice you to sin. "Watch and pray so that you will not fall into temptation," said Jesus (Matthew 26:41). Which do you think is easier, slugging it out against burning temptations or avoiding situations where temptation is likely to strike? Obviously the easiest battle is the one not begun. It's not cowardly to run away from temptation. It's wise.

But you won't be able to avoid temptation all the time. You live in a sinful world, and sin lives in you. Your heart is a professional con artist, deceiving you time after time into thinking you can walk on the edge of compromise without falling. Consequently, even though you do your best to avoid temptation, you'll need a more aggressive strategy than this to win the battle against sin.

---

2 Briefly describe one temptation you face on a fairly regular basis.

(Has God shown you a way to avoid this temptation?)

Strategy #2: Put Sin to Death

What would have become of Butch Wyman had he taken a casual approach to his predicament? He never would have lived to tell about it. Immediate, radical action was his only hope for survival. It's no exaggeration to say the health of your life with Christ requires the same radical action against sin:

Meditate on Romans 8:13. Every Christian is called to be an executioner!

Put to death, therefore, whatever belongs to your earthly nature: sexual immorality, impurity, lust, evil desires and greed, which is idolatry. Because of these, the wrath of God is coming. You used to walk in these ways, in the life you once lived. But now you must rid yourselves of all such things as these: anger, rage, malice, slander, and filthy language from your lips. (Colossians 3:5-8)

"Put to death"—it's a violent phrase, isn't it? Paul wasn't playing around with the Colossians when he wrote this to them. He wanted them to deal ruthlessly with sin. To hate it with God's hatred. To take every precaution against it, and when it got the best of them, to confess their sin to others and repent earnestly before God. Whatever form it took, and regardless of how much it might hurt, Paul urged the Colossians to cut sin out of their lives so they could live in the freedom Christ had purchased for them on the Cross.

There's a term for putting sin to death: *mortification*. Like the Colossians, each of us must mortify indwelling sin in order to mature in God and bear fruit for his glory.

> **"** Sin will not otherwise die, but by being gradually and constantly weakened; spare it, and it heals its wounds, and recovers strength.[9] **"**
> —**John Owen**

"The well-being of the Christian depends on mortification," writes Sinclair Ferguson. "Sin must be put to death in him, if he is to enjoy the comfort of the gospel and energy in his spiritual life."[10]

Do you want to experience this energy in your spiritual life? More importantly, do you want to please the One who has saved you and brought you to himself? He *expects* you to grow in holiness. And because sin is the enemy of holiness, you must put it to death. Don't expect it to surrender peacefully.

One of the most exciting things you can look forward to as a Christian is triumphing over sins. As you "fight the good fight," by God's grace you can steadily reduce the force and frequency of temptations that once overpowered you. However, none of us can hope to see sin completely destroyed until we reach heaven. As soon as you claim victory in one area, another sin will crop up ready for attack. Mortification is a lifelong commitment—and it's one you have to make if you're serious about following Christ.

Strategy #3: Bring Righteousness to Life

Avoiding temptation and attacking sin are essential strategies. But once the enemy is beaten back, there's a third strategy you must use if you hope to keep sin at bay. It involves the deliberate effort to replace sinful actions by developing righteous actions in their place. Let's look again at a passage we saw in the previous study:

> You were taught, with regard to your former way of life, to *put off* your old self, which is being corrupted by its deceitful desires; to be made new in the attitude of your minds; and to *put on* the new self created to be like God in true righteousness and holiness. (Ephesians 4:22-24)

For Further Study:
How can you prove that you are a disciple of Jesus? (See John 15:1-8, especially verse 8.)

Taking off the bad is only half of your task; Scripture calls you to work just as hard (with the Holy Spirit's help) at clothing yourself with the good.

For example, consider the sin of pride. If you really want to overcome in this area, don't just concentrate on what you're doing wrong. Do what's right! Humble yourself daily and practice treating others as if they are better, wiser, and more gifted than you are (Philippians 2:3).

Do you want to get rid of impure thoughts? Then in addition to repenting of bad thoughts, fill your mind with *good* thoughts. "Whatever is true, whatever is noble, whatever is right, whatever is pure, whatever is lovely, whatever is admirable—if anything is excellent or praiseworthy— think about such things" (Philippians 4:8).

> ❝ It were an easy thing to be a Christian, if religion stood only in a few outward works and duties. But to take the soul to task, and to deal roundly with our own hearts, and to let conscience have its full work, and to bring the soul into spiritual subjection unto God—this is not so easy a matter.[11] ❞
>
> —**Richard Sibbes**

I'll mention one final example. Perhaps you're bitter about something done to you in the past. You won't win the battle if you simply renounce that wrong attitude. You need to replace it with a godly attitude. Extend forgiveness to that woman who hurt you. Grant mercy to the guy who was merciless. Overcome evil with good.

The outworking of the Christian life in its simplest form is this: "putting off" evil and "putting on" good. These new virtues won't appear naturally, however. You will desperately need help from above. But as you grow in your relationship with the Lord, you can expect to see your life yielding more and more of "the fruit of the Spirit"—love, joy, peace, patience, kindness, goodness, faithfulness, gentleness, and self-control (Galatians 5:22-23). This is maturity. This is growth. This is what God expects of us all.

---

3 Below you'll find a list of "Vices" and "Virtues." Draw a line connecting each vice to the virtue which would best replace it.

Vices	Virtues
Depression	Serving
Laziness	Trust
Complaining	Generosity
Greed	Joy
Gossip	Thanksgiving
Anxiety	Encouragement

Our Other Enemies

If you have been a Christian more than a day or two, you have already realized that following God isn't easy. It's a battle. Despite the life, joy, and sense of purpose you've experienced, there are moments when it seems virtually impossible to do what God says you should do.

As we have seen, your biggest deterrent to obeying God is the sin within you. Sin isn't something created in you by other people. Outside circumstances can't force you to do evil. Sin is a traitor lodged in your own heart, waiting for a chance to express itself. And you are called to put it to death by the power of God's Spirit and Word.

But you face other enemies, too. As you seek to live a holy life for Christ, you can expect opposition from the world, the flesh, and the devil. Let's look at each in turn.

The World

When the Bible speaks of "the world," it is usually referring to society and culture rather than the spinning ball we call Earth. The Greek word, *kosmos*, appears over 200 times. Lawrence Richards explains its meaning in *The Expositors' Dictionary of Bible Words*:

> As a theological term, *kosmos* portrays human society as a system warped by sin, tormented by beliefs and desires and emotions that surge blindly and uncontrollably. The world system is a dark system (Ephesians 6:12), operating on basic principles that are not of God (Colossians 2:20, 1 John 2:16). The entire system lies under the power of Satan (1 John 5:19) and constitutes the kingdom from which believers are delivered by Christ (Colossians 1:13-14).[12]

Our society is not driven by a passion to glorify God. I doubt that surprises you. Executives at MTV and Universal Studios and *People* magazine and the National Football League are not meeting behind closed doors at this moment brainstorming new ways to draw you closer to God. Society's agenda revolves around self-fulfillment and pleasure. Consequently, the world's priorities and goals typically conflict with those God has for you.

Meditate on James 4:4. Have you ever thought you were being God's friend and the world's friend at the same time?

"Do not love the world or anything in the world," wrote the apostle John. "If anyone loves the world, the love of the Father is not in him" (1 John 2:15). God's kingdom and this world's system are totally opposed. That's why the Bible says, "Do not conform any longer to the pattern of this world, but be transformed by the renewing of your mind" (Romans 12:2). As a follower of Jesus Christ, you're to be "in the world"—a bold, influential witness for Jesus Christ—but not "of the world" (John 17:11-16). Rather than adopting the values and priorities of the godless world around you, recognize them as enemy propaganda, and recommit yourself to living for the kingdom of God.

The Flesh

In centuries past, some Christian sects have mistakenly believed the human body is evil. Nowhere does the Bible say that your skin, hair, bones, and organs are wicked. However, within you is something the Bible calls "the flesh" or "the sinful nature" (depending on what translation you use). Whether you know it by that name or not, the flesh is certainly no stranger to you. You could think of it as your capacity for sin, your propensity for evil. It's the part of you that responds so readily to worldly enticements while resisting the inner work of the Holy Spirit. In fact, your flesh battles the Spirit for control over your mind, will, and affections. Galatians 5:17 says, "For the sinful nature [the flesh] desires what is contrary to the Spirit, and the Spirit what is contrary to the sinful nature. They are in conflict with each other, so that you do not do what you want."

Resisting the world's influences is difficult enough; doing battle against the flesh takes great discernment and perseverance. Here are four manifestations of the flesh you can expect to encounter.

> **" [The Christian] must be willing to give up every habit and practice which is wrong in God's sight. He must set his face against it, quarrel with it, break off from it, fight with it, crucify it and labour to keep it under, whatever the world around him may say or think...He and sin must quarrel, if he and God are to be friends.**[13] **"**
>
> **—J.C. Ryle**

Self-centeredness. From a fleshly perspective, you are the center of the universe. Your reputation, ambitions, feelings, appetites, ideas, and preferences are its chief concern. Your flesh loves to pamper itself and impress others. It does not respond well to the motto Jesus gave: "The man who loves his life will lose it, while the man who hates his life in this world will keep it for eternal life...My Father will honor the one who serves me" (John 12:25,26). In order to master your self-centered flesh, you will need to stop exalting yourself and learn to put the Lord and others first.

Self-sufficiency. The flesh is confident in its ability to do anything, even to fight sin and live for God. Peter, one of Jesus' closest disciples and friends, insisted he would never deny the Lord. But on the night of the Lord's arrest, Peter did deny him—not just once, but three times. His self-confidence got him in deep yogurt.

Meditate on Proverbs 3:5-6. Who is—and isn't—worthy of your confidence?

"Cursed is the one who trusts in man," said the prophet Jeremiah, "who depends on flesh for his strength and whose heart turns away from the Lord" (Jeremiah 17:5). Trusting in your own ability is both foolish and proud. But God will be pleased as you humble yourself and live each day depending on the help and strength of the Lord.

Self-righteousness. Jesus reserved his sharpest rebukes for the Pharisees and Sadducees. These self-righteous hypocrites considered themselves spiritually superior to everyone else. That's what the flesh will do to you. It will cause you to criticize the tiniest faults in others while letting major sins in your own life go unchallenged (Matthew 7:3-5). Here are some other common symptoms of fleshly self-righteousness: being more aware of your virtues than you are of your sins; judging others more harshly than you judge yourself; wanting God to punish others (especially those who have hurt you) while expecting him to have mercy on you; and justifying sinful actions or attitudes toward people who have sinned against you. If any of these shoes fit, recognize that your self-righteous flesh is at work.

---

4 Fill in the blanks for the following verse, taken from the New International Version of the Bible:

"For in the same way you _____ others, you will

be _____, and with the_____ you

use, it will be _____ to you." (Matthew 7:2)

Self-gratification. Your flesh is determined to satisfy all its appetites on a regular basis. It aims to get whatever it wants—extra sleep, nicer clothes, an exotic vacation, chocolate cheesecake, you name it. But as a follower of Christ, you are no longer a slave to your appetites:

> Those who belong to Christ Jesus have crucified the sinful nature [flesh] with its passions and desires. Since we live by the Spirit, let us keep in step with the Spirit.... (Galatians 5:24-25)

For Further Study: What's the difference between the two lifestyles described in Ephesians 4:17-24?

Instead of yielding to your flesh, you are to control it. Instead of pampering your flesh, you are to crucify it. This doesn't mean you can never eat a piece of cheesecake again. But instead of living to satisfy your sinful passions as you once did, you are now taking up your Cross daily in order to become like the holy One in whose footsteps you follow (Luke 9:23-24).

The Devil

Your final enemy is the devil, or Satan (a name that means "adversary"). Satan hates God and opposes God's people. He is a real personality—not just a red-suited, pitchfork-wielding figment of someone's imagination. The Bible refers to him repeatedly as someone with vast power to do evil. Tony Sargent writes,

> Evil is incarnated in Satan. The world, in which he has taken up residence, is infested with his emissaries....What is more, the devil picks out the Church as an object of hate. Individual Christians are in the firing line. Satan's goal is to eliminate the glory of God, to undo the work the Lord achieved on the Cross. Christians should consider themselves as involved in mortal combat with the enemy of their souls.[14]

For Further Study:
The Devil goes by many different names—see Matthew 4:10; Luke 11:18; John 8:44, 10:10; 2 Corinthians 11:14; and Revelation 12:9-10.

What does Satan do? How does he operate? "We are not unaware of his schemes," wrote Paul (2 Corinthians 2:11). He **prowls** like a lion, looking to devour the unsuspecting (1 Peter 5:8). He **deceives** those who stray from the truth (Revelation 12:9). He **tempts** the saints to sin against God (Matthew 4:3). He **schemes** against God and seeks to outwit God's people (2 Corinthians 2:11). He **lies** and distorts the truth (John 8:44). He also **accuses** us day and night (Revelation 12:10) and tries to weaken our confidence in God's saving grace. These are just a handful of Satan's malicious strategies.

In order for you to be victorious in the battle, it's vital that you understand Satan's strengths. But it's equally important that you understand his limitations. As you'll quickly see, he is no match for God.

Satan is not all-powerful. There is a fixed limit to his dark and heinous deeds. Any thought of God and Satan duking it out like two super heavyweights is ludicrous. The devil is far more powerful than any man, but he doesn't even begin to match up to God Omnipotent.

> **"** Satan shall not need to tempt him much who has already tempted himself.[15] **"**
>
> —**Obadiah Sedgwick**

Satan is not all-knowing. Though crafty, cunning, and highly deceptive, Satan lacks the infinite knowledge and wisdom of God. "We should not think that demons can know the future or that they can read our minds or know our thoughts," states theologian Wayne Grudem.[16]

Satan is not present everywhere at the same time. He admittedly gets around a lot quicker than we do, but he himself cannot be in the demonic temples of Tibet and in my kitchen at the same time. He has to leave one to reach the other. This is good news because it means you and I will probably never encounter a bold, frontal assault from Satan himself. Frankly, most of us just aren't that high up on his priority list. Yet in his service are hordes of ministering demons who inflict much agony, bondage, and grief on the saints of God.

Take Your Stand!

It would be foolish and dangerous to minimize Satan's threat. He is real and he is deadly. However, countless Christians make the opposite mistake and *exaggerate* Satan's threat. Many become so preoccupied with fighting him and his demons that they lose sight of the power and presence of God. They are wasting precious energy. For the wonderful fact is that Jesus has already defeated Satan and his demonic hordes.

Colossians 2:15 says of our Lord, "And having disarmed the powers and authorities, he made a public spectacle of them, triumphing over them by the cross." A study note in *The NIV Study Bible* fleshes out the full meaning of Paul's words:

> The picture is of conquered soldiers stripped of their clothes as well as their weapons to symbolize their total defeat…The metaphor recalls a Roman general leading his captives through the streets of his city for all the citizens to see as evidence of his complete victory….[17]

Jesus has dealt Satan a crushing, final defeat. His goose is literally cooked, as we see in the Book of Revelation: "And the devil, who deceived them, was thrown into the lake of burning sulfur, where the beast and the false prophet had been thrown. They [including all of Satan's demons] will be tormented day and night for ever and ever" (Revelation 20:10).

Meditate on Romans 16:20. Because Jesus has defeated Satan, you share in the victory!

The fact that Satan has not yet been eradicated from this planet is not a sign of his power. Rather, it is a sign of God's sovereignty. The Lord will allow Satan access to the earth only so far as it serves his ultimate plan.

Satan is not outwitting God, nor forcing him into some type of cosmic stalemate. It would take but a single word from the mouth of our Lord to overthrow the devil and his entire kingdom. They would be devastated in an instant. Once God chooses to carry out his sentence, Satan and his demonic minions will not trouble us for one millisecond longer.

But, in his sovereign and omnipotent wisdom, God allows our enemy to remain active for a little while longer. And without exaggerating his power, we are to wage war against Satan and his works. You will not get to show your colors against him in heaven, for he will not be there. Only in this lifetime can you win glory for your King by displaying valor against his enemy.

---

5 A smart soldier can often anticipate an enemy attack and prepare for it. As you look at the coming week, do you see any potential demonic ambushes in the making? (Examples: extra stress at work; lunch appointment with someone who thinks you're nuts for believing in Jesus, etc.)

(What preparations can you make now to beat the enemy?)

"Put on the full armor of God," Paul exhorts us, "so that you can take your stand against the devil's schemes." What is that armor? You'll find it described piece by piece in Ephesians 6:10-18, a classic passage on spiritual warfare. Though we'll touch on it just briefly, take some time this week to reflect more on this passage.

The belt of truth. Paul is not referring to doctrinal truth or biblical knowledge, but rather to a lifestyle of truth, or integrity. Satan's inroads into your life will be greatly limited as you walk uprightly before God and man.

For Further Study:
How does Satan use our sins to his advantage? (See Ephesians 4:26-27)

The breastplate of righteousness. Serious character deficiencies will make you vulnerable to demonic attack. But the opposite is also true: dagger thrusts of temptation can't easily pierce the one devoted to the holiness of God.

The "shoes" of the gospel of peace. There is no better way to combat the accuser than to remind yourself that Jesus Christ has died for your sins. Jerry Bridges says we need to "preach the gospel to ourselves every day."[18]

The shield of faith. Your faith must not rest on your own righteousness or on other believers, but on God. He is all-powerful. He is totally good. He is absolutely sovereign. The more you know and trust him, the less Satan's lies will influence you.

> ❝ Few things afford the Christian such relief and encouragement as the memory of sins which once ruled him, but which he has conquered by the power of the Spirit of God.[19] ❞
>
> —J.I. Packer

The helmet of salvation. Salvation is more than being forgiven. It is being freed from the power and penalty of sin. Remind yourself daily that you are no longer a servant of sin because you have been born again and united with Christ.

The sword of the Spirit (the Word of God). This is the only piece of armor listed that can be used to attack. God's Word is powerful! As you meditate on it, hiding its truth in your heart, the Holy Spirit will help you wield it well against the enemy.

Butch Wyman knew how to wield a blade in an hour of crisis. Do you? God calls you to battle against the world, the flesh, the devil, and your own indwelling sin. This is no time to be passive. Stand strong—and fight hard—in the power of the Lord. ■

GROUP DISCUSSION

1. Your home is on fire! You only have time to rescue the three possessions you value most. What would you take?

2. Where does sin originate?

3. For the *third* time this week your spouse has locked the keys in the car. You explode: "That makes me soooo *mad!*" According to this study, what really caused your anger?

4. Discuss how you could flee one specific temptation.

5. Can you think of any sins God has helped you conquer? If appropriate, give the details.

6. What do you think might happen to a Christian who "put off" sin but never "put on" righteousness?

7. How can a Christian live in the world without loving the world? Try to come up with specific examples.

8. Are there any sins you are reluctant to give up?

9. How would you have rated Satan's power before reading this study? (0 = "Underestimated" and 5 = "Overestimated.")

10. Do you feel equipped for the battle?

The Practice of Godliness by Jerry Bridges (Colorado Springs, CO: NavPress, 1983)

The Discipline of Grace by Jerry Bridges (Colorado Springs, CO: NavPress, 1994)

Pleasing God by R.C. Sproul (Wheaton, IL: Tyndale House Publishers, 1988)

Sin and Temptation by John Owen (Carlisle, PA: The Banner of Truth Trust, 1967) Though not light reading, this Puritan classic is unrivaled on the subject of understanding and battling sin.

Answer to Warm-Up
(from page 69): A four-year study done by the National Research Council predicts that all of these items will be standard issue for U.S. Army troops by the year 2020…except the last one; the Army has not yet found a way to duplicate *Star Trek*'s electronic cloaking devices. (Source: William Matthews, "The Troops of 2020," Army Times Publishing Company, 11/13/94)

WHERE DO WE GO FROM HERE?

BIBLE STUDY Colossians 3:1-3

WARM-UP Which of the following Olympic sports do you think demands the most training from its athletes?

A. Archery

B. Badminton

C. Boxing

D. Canoeing/Kayaking

E. Cycling

F. Diving

H. Luge

(See page 101 for answer)

PERSONAL STUDY Standing over his casket was the most wrenching thing I had ever done. I felt such loss. Such respect. I touched his cold, stiff hand and studied his wrinkled face. He was the most Christlike man I had ever known. Though he stood only 5'6" and weighed 136 pounds, John Shank was a spiritual giant.

My grandfather's greatest dream was to go to school. He grew up on a "one cow farm" in the Shenandoah Valley, surrounded by Mennonite families like his own. From as early as he could remember, young John longed for the day he could attend the old clapboard schoolhouse with his friends and learn about the rest of the world. His education was postponed, however, by a family tragedy.

One morning John, age six, went to fetch something in the barn. Rounding the corner, he found his dad lying face down in a puddle of water. Motionless. He had suffered an epileptic seizure, the doctor concluded, apparently brought on by a kick in the head from their mule two weeks earlier. He drowned in two inches of water.

> ❝ A look at abandoned tombstones with names no one remembers is a stark reminder of our eventual anonymity in this world. What do you know about your great-grandfather? What will your great-grandchildren know about you?[1] ❞
>
> —**Randy Alcorn**

With his father's death, young John learned how to struggle with grief and disappointment. His mother worked sunup to sundown keeping the place together and her eight children fed and clothed. She was deeply devoted to God, her church, and her family, and she did the very best she could. But she had to do it alone. She never remarried.

Eventually the family adjusted to the loss, and John was allowed to attend school. I still have a cracked, antique photograph of Grandpa as a 10-year-old boy sitting on the edge of his seat in that little school room. His eyes look wide as saucers, drinking in everything he possibly could. He was a fine student. His passion for learning was finally given the chance to grow. His whole world began opening up to him through the wonder of education.

It only lasted a couple of years, though. John's mother realized that in order to keep things running, she needed his help at home. He cried the day his dream came to an end. But he obeyed his mom, taking an extra share of the household responsibilities on his young shoulders. He didn't attend another day of school for the rest of his life.

Several years after Grandpa died, I spoke with his one remaining brother. Uncle Emmanuel's mind and memory were still sharp at age 88. "John was the best of the bunch," he said. "Everyone loved him. Never once did he backslide in his devotion to the Lord. Never a harsh word. He was so different from the rest of us." The more Uncle Emmanuel spoke, the more I realized just what a man of character my grandfather had been.

Meditate on Romans 5:3-4. What good can you expect to come out of suffering?

Grandpa was the most selfless servant you could ever hope to meet. He faithfully cared for his sister Maggie as arthritis crippled her and twisted her in knots. He served his own children, who for years rejected their Christian upbringing. As they reaped the consequences of their sin Grandpa was there with love, bags of groceries, money, acceptance, godly counsel, and tear-stained prayers. When he was in his 70s he told us he hoped "momma," as he affectionately called my grandmother, would "go home" first. He prayed daily that he could outlive her. Why? Because more than half a century earlier he had vowed to cherish and take care of his wife, and he knew he wouldn't be able to fulfill that vow if he died first.

For Further Study: If you had to name the three most important qualities in a person, would your answer be the same as in 1 Corinthians 13:13?

In 1977 God answered his prayers. His beloved Irene—the cute little girl I can spot in Grandpa's school photo, smiling on the other side of the classroom as if she knew she was going to be his bride—now lay in her own casket. "Isn't she beautiful?" he whispered as he stood over her for the last time. "She's just as beautiful as the day I married her."

He passed away two years later. After his funeral, as I was going through his things, I came across the last birthday card he had given his beloved. In his own shaky handwriting he had written these lines:

Hi Mom,

> So you have another birthday. Yes they keep coming. Yes we have travelled a long way together, over rough places and smooth, over mountain tops and deep valleys. Yes we have experienced heat and cold, we have seen dark clouds and bright sunshine, but through it all we have weathered the storms together. And were it my lot to cease life as it is, and start all over, and had I a hundred from which to choose, I would by-pass 99 and choose the one I chose 55 years ago. Sincerely, with love,

> Daddy

---

1 What would you like people to remember about you when you pass away? (Check any that apply.)

❑ Your position of influence in local politics

❑ The immaculate condition of your rose beds and lawn

❑ Your devotion to family and friends

❑ Your laughter and enthusiasm for life

❑ The way you took care of your fingernails

❑ Your love for God and his Word

❑ The price you paid for your new Jacuzzi

Recounting my grandfather's life of service would take a book in itself. I have never met anyone who had a cross word to say about him. Before and after his funeral, numerous people who had known him or worked with him referred to his loving, Christlike disposition.

What few of them realized was that for the last 30 years of his life he had maintained that godly disposition despite daily, agonizing headaches. The painful pounding would wake him up around 4 a.m. each morning. Then, after a couple of pills and a cold compress, he caught another hour or so of sleep if he was lucky. (His family always wondered if he had a tumor, but when he died they couldn't bring themselves to request an autopsy.)

Headaches weren't his only hardship. During the years he work as a janitor at a Mennonite college (how he loved to be around school!) he lost his left eye in a freak accident. He was pushing a spring back into a sofa one day when it slipped from under his thumb and shot straight through his glasses, blinding him immediately. But no one ever heard him complain about it. Even in his hardest moments, he displayed the quiet strength of character forged during a lifetime of loving God.

> ❝ He therefore is the devout man, who lives no longer to his own will, or the way and spirit of the world, but to the sole will of God, who considers God in everything, who serves God in everything, who makes all the parts of his common life, parts of piety, by doing everything in the name of God, and under such rules as are conformable to His glory.[2] ❞
>
> —**William Law**

Did he sin? Of course. Was he aware of his sin? Overly so. Listening to him confess the evil in his heart, you might have thought he was Jack the Ripper. Was he aware of his daily need for a Savior, for the ever-effective blood of the Lamb to cleanse his wretched soul? To answer that question, you only needed to stand beside him on a Sunday morning during worship at Weaver's Mennonite Church. (He served as a deacon there for over 50 years.) I doubt anyone has ever sung with less skill and more heart the classic words, "Amazing grace, how sweet the sound, that saved a wretch like me...." Grandpa wasn't just singing. He was adoring.

There were no letters after his name when he died. No degrees. No honors. No fancy titles. He didn't even finish grade school. But to the neighbors and friends and co-workers who lined up at the house to pay their last respects, he was the most godly man they had ever met.

Meditate on Matthew 20:25-28. How does God measure greatness?

All who knew my grandfather knew a great life had finally come to an end. From his boyhood conversion to his final coronation, he had lived for the glory of God. Now his body rests beside his beloved Irene while he joins all the worshipers of generations past in exalting and praising God—with two good eyes and no headaches.

Why have I shared in such detail about a poor, simple man whose death went unnoticed by most of the world? To get you to think about what will matter on the day of *your* death. How will people talk about you when you are hard and cold? More importantly, what will God say about you? What will he point to as the consuming preoccupation of your life?

Living for the Glory of God

In the final moments before your death, I can pretty much guarantee you won't be thinking about building an addition on your house, buying a new sports car, putting in extra time on the job, upgrading your carpets, or taking a cruise on the Mediterranean. You may have poured time and money into these things while you lived, but they won't seem very important at the threshold of death. Instead, I think you'll be reflecting on the way you have spent your life, and whether you've invested yourself in things that really matter.

> ❝ Remembrance of death acts like a filter, helping us to hold on to the essential and let go of the trivial...What men or women in their right mind would continue an affair if they really believed they might not wake up in the morning? What person would risk entering eternity in a drunken stupor? What fool would ignore his loved ones and God for one last night so that he could make another quick ten thousand just before he died?[4] ❞
>
> **—Gary Thomas**

What *are* the things that matter? What is the purpose of your existence? Centuries ago, a group of church leaders met to discuss matters of the faith and gave a brilliant answer to this question. It is both profound and precise: "Man's chief end is to glorify God and to enjoy him forever."[3] Material pleasures pale beside the privilege of glorifying God and enjoying a deepening relationship with him. This is what you were made for. This is a vocation worthy of your time, energy, and deepest passion.

"Whatever you do," the Bible says, "do it all for the glory of God" (1 Corinthians 10:31). You want to please God, right? Then memorize this verse and meditate on what it means. A commitment to do *all* for the glory of God has far-reaching implications. It will influence every decision you make, every word you speak, every purchase you consider. It will reduce life's many decisions to two basic options: Are you going to do what brings you the most personal pleasure, or do what brings God the greatest glory?

For Further Study:
Read 1 Corinthians
7:29-31. What is hap-
pening to the world?
How should that affect
the way we view materi-
al possessions?

As you would expect, decisions that bring God the most glory are rarely the easiest choices. You won't naturally be inclined to forgive the person who slandered you behind your back. Your flesh probably won't encourage you to make financial sacrifices in order to support the mission of your local church. The daily decision to "put off" sin and "put on" Christlike virtues will be so difficult, in fact, that you would never be able to do it apart from the power of the Holy Spirit.

Difficult though it may be, living for the glory of God should be the most fundamental motivation of your life. To glorify God means you choose to elevate his will over your own, regardless of personal cost. It means you choose to exalt him by your worship and obedience. It means you choose to live in such a way that other people see Christ in you. It means you choose to follow the example of Jesus, who devoted his entire life to honoring and glorifying his Father. Paul summed it up when he wrote that Christians "should no longer live for themselves but for him who died for them and was raised again" (2 Corinthians 5:15).

> ❧ It ought to be the business of every day to prepare for our last day.[5] 🔢
>
> **—Matthew Henry**

---

2 In the space below, describe one thing God has asked you to do that will require some degree of sacrifice.

Living for the glory of God is a daily choice. Actually, it's a choice we make every second. I am amazed at how often I can begin a day in the Lord's presence, expressing my desire to please him in every situation, and then find myself angry toward someone that afternoon, or irritated by a traffic jam. As you face life's twists and turns, count on one thing being constant: your flesh will always seek its own way. Every day is an arena in which to live for God's glory or coddle your selfish interests.

Let's get practical for a minute. Whom can you forgive today—right now? To what undeserving person can you extend mercy and love simply because you want to glorify God? What area of selfishness can you begin to attack until it has become a selfless reflection of Jesus?

Meditate on John 8:49-50. Though Jesus had every right to exalt himself, whose glory did he seek?

What has the Holy Spirit been exposing in your life? Anger? Self-pity? Unbridled pursuit of fame and fortune? Rebellion toward your parents? Pride and selfishness with your spouse? Gossip and backbiting? Lustful looks, or worse? Submit to the Spirit's conviction and make the hard choices. Beginning today, "make no provision for the flesh in regard to its lusts" (Romans 13:14, NAS). Every time you "put off" a sinful craving and "put on" a Christ-like virtue in its place, you bring glory and honor to the Lord who died for you. Being transformed into the likeness of Jesus Christ is your lifelong occupation. Embrace it with a passion!

> 66 The glory of God is a silver thread which must run through all our actions.[6] 99
>
> —**Thomas Watson**

Living for the glory of God means dying to the desires of self. Is that going to be fun and fascinating? No. Is God worthy of it? Yes. That's why every true Christian will make this a daily resolution.

A few years ago, I penned in my journal some personal confessions about living for God's glory. Just because I've got them down on paper doesn't mean I've mastered each of these. But maybe these will inspire you, as they have me, to keep seeking God's glory in all circumstances.

■ When sorrow and disappointment press deeply on my heart and soul, I'll say, *Your glory is my highest goal.*

■ When it requires my utmost resolve to deny myself and lay down my life for others, so be it—*Your glory is my highest goal.*

■ When commanded to forgive though I would rather retaliate; when eager to see my adversaries receive judgment rather than mercy; help me stop and ask, *Is your glory my highest goal?*

■ When I would prefer that others sympathize with my shortcomings rather than challenge me to obey your Word, remind me that *your glory is my highest goal.*

■ When my serving and sacrifice are met with criticism or a demand for more, may I say nevertheless, *Your glory is my highest goal.*

For Further Study: For a few of the reasons why God is worthy of all glory, see Revelation 4:11, 5:12, and 15:4.

■ When I'm bombarded by temptations to gratify my flesh, and being like Christ is the last thing I want, help me to remember—*Your glory is my highest goal.*

■ When my heart covets the praise of others and I want to be told that my accomplishments are significant and indispensable, dear God, help me repent of such arrogance! *Your glory is my highest goal.*

■ When I experience painful or puzzling circumstances and life's path seems to lead through dark valleys more often than mountain peaks, may I remain steadfast in this resolve: *Your glory is my highest goal.*

■ When tempted to fear the opinions of man more than the dread of dishonoring and displeasing you, may I do your bidding—no matter how unpopular—because *your glory is my highest goal.*

■ When things are going well and my life is filled with the blessings of God, may I not set my heart on them, for *your glory is my highest goal.*

■ When I'd rather settle into a comfortable routine than pioneer onward in your advancing kingdom, remind me that comfort and convenience aren't the issue, for *your glory is my highest goal.*

■ And on that final day of judgment, when all I can boast of is the merciful work of Jesus on my behalf...when all I have been, all I have said, all I have wanted, and all I have done receive the piercing assessment of your holy scrutiny...if possible, Lord, by your grace, may I hear you say, "Well done, my son. You have made my heart glad, for I saw that *my glory was your highest goal.*"

---

3 What is one situation that is currently testing your commitment to "do all for the glory of God"? In the space below, write out a resolution similar to those listed above. (Example: "Even when I wake up and realize it's destined to be a bad hair day, help me praise you anyway, for your *glory is my highest goal.*")

Taking Your Place in a Local Church

A Christian can't hope to glorify God and live a life worthy of him apart from committed involvement in a church. But not everyone understands this, as Jack Hayford has observed:

> She was sweet, beautifully simple and obviously sensitive. She had signed the visitor's guestbook in the foyer of the church, and I read her entry following the service, positioning myself at the door to greet the worshipers as they left. Beside her name, she had indicated as her church home, "The Body of Christ," and for the location of her church, "Worldwide."
>
> I chuckled to myself as I glanced at her entry, but felt regret over the hollowness of the idea represented by this sincere young believer. It isn't uncommon to find people whose notion of membership in the Church is equally ethereal. And the saddest part is that such uncommitment is regarded by many as being of the highest order of spirituality.[7]

Meditate on Hebrews 10:24-25. Why is it important for believers to meet together as the church?

Christians are unique. They are different from any other group of people in the world because they are being assembled and joined together by God to become "a dwelling in which God lives by his Spirit" (Ephesians 2:22). While God certainly loves and lives in individual believers, "the Christian life is inescapably corporate."[8] Let me share five reasons why participation in a local church is essential for your spiritual growth.

> **"** Truth without emotion produces dead orthodoxy and a church full (or half-full) of artificial admirers (like people who write generic anniversary cards for a living). On the other hand, emotion without truth produces empty frenzy and cultivates shallow people who refuse the discipline of rigorous thought. But true worship comes from people who are deeply emotional and who love deep and sound doctrine. Strong affections for God rooted in truth are the bone and marrow of biblical worship.[9] **"**
>
> —**John Piper**

Worship. When God's people gather, exalting God should be their highest priority. This is the essence of worship, though its forms will vary. You can worship God with a 16th-century hymn or a contemporary band. Both communion and the confession of sin are acts of worship, as is the preaching (and hearing) of God's Word.

God seeks those who will worship him "in spirit and truth" (John 4:23). What does this mean? That your worship "must have heart and head," as John Piper puts it. "Worship must engage emotions and thought."[10] Lifeless knowledge doesn't please God—but neither does enthusiastic heresy. He wants to see your head and heart working together as you worship with his saints.

Service. As part of the church, you have the privilege of helping meet the needs of others. But the biggest need you meet may be your own, for unless you learn to serve, you will never become like your Lord. This was one of his most distinguishing characteristics. And as he proved by word and example, the highway to greatness in the kingdom of God leads through the valley of humble service. It is difficult to serve in isolation. But within the church, you become a "supporting ligament" that helps the whole body grow and mature (Ephesians 4:16).

For Further Study:
If you want to be like Jesus, how will you need to treat other Christians? (See John 13:3-5,12-17)

---

4 What abilities and interests has God given you that could be used for serving in your church?

❏ Administration ❏ Teaching ❏ Graphic design

❏ Serving the needy ❏ Evangelism ❏ Landscaping

❏ Financial counseling ❏ Writing ❏ Computer skills

❏ Children's ministry ❏ Music ❏ Hospitality

❏ Facility maintenance ❏ Drama ❏ Other_____

Growth. If you could prepare for heaven the way a college student prepares for final exams, you might be able to do it on your own in some dusty corner of the local library. But Christian maturity involves a lot more than obtaining knowledge. It requires that you *apply* that knowledge. Your growth in love, humility, patience, gentleness, service, and numerous other areas can only occur in the context of committed relationships. Where? In the church, spurred on by the example, encouragement, and even the provocation of others.

> ❝ If the church is central to God's purpose, as seen in both history and the gospel, it must surely also be central to our lives. How can we take lightly what God takes so seriously? How dare we push to the circumference what God has placed at the center?[11] ❞
>
> —John R.W. Stott

Training. To live a spiritually fruitful life, you need to be equipped for service. Church isn't like a hospital or law firm where you leave all the work to the "professionals." Instead, church leaders have the responsibility

> ...to prepare God's people for works of service, so that the body of Christ may be built up until we all reach unity in the faith and in the knowledge of the Son of God and become mature, attaining to the whole measure of the fullness of Christ. (Ephesians 4:12-13)

Meditate on 1 Corinthians 12:7. Does God limit church ministry to a handful of leaders?

Their job is to train *you*, not do all the work themselves! Though seminaries and parachurch ministries offer many types of specialized training, the local church is the main context where Christians are to be trained for kingdom service. The classroom can't expose character flaws half so effectively as the nitty-gritty of church life does, nor can it give you the same wealth of opportunities to lay down your life and serve others.

Witnessing. Some Christians have a deep, aggressive compassion for the lost. They compulsively share their faith with others. Is that you? I wish it were me. There are times when I feel a wave of intense concern for certain individuals, and I try to respond in faith, trusting that God is letting me feel his heart for a person in a particular situation. But on a typical day, I'm not terribly overwhelmed with remorse for the lost people around me.

> ❝ We do not evangelize because we want to, or because we like to, or because we feel like it. We evangelize because we have been told to. ❞
>
> —Billy Graham

And yet it became clear to me some years ago that in witnessing, as with everything else in my life, I needed to be motivated by the glory of God instead of my personal preference. I began to see how even awkward attempts to share my testimony with non-Christians, to pray for them, or to give them my personal testimony tract or a church invitation brought glory to God. This has changed my perspective on evangelism. It's all for God's glory. A solid church will encourage you in evangelism, equip you for evangelism, and—most importantly—provide a place where those God reaches through your evangelism can be nurtured and built up in the faith.

For Further Study: Two passages in which God commissions us to evangelize are Matthew 28:19-20 and 2 Corinthians 5:18-20.

God saved you with the purpose of adding you to his body, the church. Because I have only been able to scratch the surface of this critical topic, I've recommended a book at the end of this study titled *Restoration In The Church*, by Terry Virgo. It shows why the church has a central role in God's plan for the world...and in his plan for you.

What Are You Staring At?

"Kking kr ma kon." My friend knelt beside the woman's wheelchair, trying to make out her words. He and some other members of our church were visiting Oakwood Nursing Home to lead a Christmas service for the elderly residents. As he spoke to this woman, it seemed clear she had something important to communicate.

"Kking kr ma kon," she repeated. Her head sagged back as if her neck were too weak to support it. "Kking kr ma kon."

A spasm of coughing came and went. After clearing her throat of phlegm, she was able to speak a bit more clearly. "Lkg or ma kon. Lking ffffr ma kon."

He leaned forward, trying to decipher her words. Again she strained to express her heart. "Lking for ma crn." She had a faint smile now. "Lking for ma cron."

Suddenly it hit him.

"Looking for your *crown*?" he asked.

A noticeable smile of relief passed over her face. He had understood. With those four mumbled words, she had managed to say that her eyes and heart were looking beyond the smells, beyond the medicines, beyond the weariness, and beyond the lonely hours spent staring at the same depressing sights. She had something buried deep inside that worn-out body of hers. It was called hope. She was looking forward to her crown.

Did it change her circumstances? Nope. Did it change her pitiful condition? Nope. Did it help her endure? You better believe it. And looking toward our heavenly reward will help us endure as well. For even when we stand firmly on God's promises and resist the devil's attacks, some things still won't turn out the way we want. God sometimes dips into a file called "Mystery" when developing the script of our lives. He may never allow us to understand why certain incidents occur. Try as we might, we may never get an explanation this side of eternity that fully satisfies us. Often the circumstances improve, and we go on. But what if God, for some superior yet unknown reason, lets the circumstances *deteriorate*? What can help us then?

> **"** The time is very short. A few more years of watching and praying, a few more tossings on the sea of this world, a few more deaths and changes, a few more winters and summers, and all will be over. We shall have fought our last battle, and shall need to fight no more.[12] **"**
>
> —J.C. Ryle

For Further Study:
Want to get a glimpse
of the crown that
awaits you? See James
1:12 and 1 Peter 5:4.

Perhaps we can learn from the example of this hopeful old saint at Oakwood Nursing Home. She could have retreated into a shell of self-pity. But rather than looking at her external surroundings, depressing as they were, she was looking toward the *eternal*—toward her crown. She was looking above the trials and turbulence of life and gazing toward the life to come, just like the apostle Paul, who said: "Now there is in store for me the crown of righteousness, which the Lord, the righteous Judge, will award to me on that day—and not only to me, but also to all who have longed for his appearing" (2 Timothy 4:8).

---

5 Can you think of any earthly treasure, status, or accomplishment that might rival the heavenly reward God will give those who live for his glory? (The space below has been intentionally omitted.)

One day you will stand before the God who made you. Depending on how you lived, that day will bring great joy or deep regret. Did you make it your purpose to live every day for the glory of God, regardless of personal cost? Did you pursue humility and service? Were you committed to becoming more like Christ in your thoughts, words, and actions? Were you faithful with the time and talents you had been given?

If you had to answer those questions right now, you might have to say "no." But it is not too late. There is still time to change gears. Today you can decide to live for your Creator and Father without reservation. Today you can shift your gaze and affections from the things of this world to the imperishable rewards to come. Even if you feel you have made a total mess of things, don't give up. Your yesterdays don't have to determine your todays and your tomorrows. You still have time to live a life that glorifies God.

> **"** Therefore we do not lose heart. Though outwardly we are wasting away, yet inwardly we are being renewed day by day. For our light and momentary troubles are achieving for us an eternal glory that far outweighs them all. So we fix our eyes not on what is seen, but on what is unseen. For what is seen is temporary, but what is unseen is eternal. **"**
>
> **—2 Corinthians 4:16–18**

Your pilgrimage on this earth is so short, "a mist that appears for a little while and then vanishes" (James 4:14). Yet these few brief years will determine how you spend

Meditate on Matthew 6:19-21. If you need motivation to switch your "investment strategy," look no further!

eternity. Do you want to experience reward rather than regret? Then fix your sights on the crown to come!

> Since, then, you have been raised with Christ, set your hearts on things above, where Christ is seated at the right hand of God. Set your minds on things above, not on earthly things. For you died, and your life is now hidden with Christ in God. (Colossians 3:1-3)

Richard Baxter, a Puritan pastor, said it simply: "Live this life with the hopes and fears of another life."[13] Like those heroes of the faith who have gone on before, set your heart on that day when you will stand before your God and Father in heaven. I assure you, it is a goal worthy of your constant and undistracted gaze. ■

GROUP DISCUSSION

1. Who is the most Christlike person you have ever known? What are some of the specific qualities you admire about him or her?

2. How might a hard life (like the author's grandfather experienced) lead to a *holy* life?

3. The Westminster Shorter Catechism states that man's chief end, or main purpose, is to glorify God and enjoy him forever. *Before* you became a Christian, how would you have completed this sentence? "Man's chief end is to...."

4. Can you think of a situation during the past 24 hours in which you had to choose between God's glory and your own self-interest?

5. Share your answer to Question 3 on page 94.

6. What are some of the ways *you* benefit from active involvement in your church?

7. What are some of the ways *your church* benefits from your involvement?

8. Do you agree that "the Christian life is inescapably corporate"? (Page 95) Why or why not?

9. What gives the Christian hope to endure hardship?

10. In what practical ways will you respond to this study?

RECOMMENDED READING

Restoration in the Church by Terry Virgo (Columbia, MO: Christian Fellowship of Columbia, 1989)

A Quest for Godliness by J.I. Packer (Wheaton, IL: Crossway Books, 1990)

A Body of Divinity by Thomas Watson (Carlisle, PA: The Banner of Truth Trust, 1992) This book is a gold mine of insight—in particular, it contains an excellent section on living for the glory of God.

Answer to Warm-Up
(from page 87): **Diving** competitors spend 8 hours a day, 6 days a week, and 48 weeks a year in training for the Olympics, according to 5-time Olympic coach Dick Kimball. That's a total of 2,304 hours per year. Time estimates on the other sports (in hours of training per year) are: **Canoeing/Kayaking** (2,028), **Badminton** (1,920), **Luge** (1,512), **Boxing** (1,480), **Cycling** (1,050), and **Archery** (364). (Sources: Olympic team representatives.)

NOTES   STUDY ONE – Who Makes the First Move?

1. Jerry Bridges, *Transforming Grace* (Colorado Springs, CO: NavPress, 1991), p. 73.
2. Anthony Hoekema, *Saved by Grace* (Grand Rapids, MI: William B. Eerdmans Publishing Co., 1989), p. 56.
3. A.W. Pink, *An Exposition of the Sermon On the Mount* (Grand Rapids, MI: Baker Book House, 1953), p. 16.
4. This list was adapted from John Broger, *Self-Confrontation: A Manual for In-Depth Discipleship* (Nashville, TN: Thomas Nelson Publishers, 1994), Lesson 1, p. 3.
5. Wayne Grudem, *Systematic Theology* (Grand Rapids, MI: Zondervan Publishing House, 1994), p. 693.
6. J. Norval Geldenhuys in *Basic Christian Doctrines*, edited by Carl F. H. Henry (Grand Rapids, MI: Baker Book House, 1962), p. 179.
7. Wayne Grudem, *Systematic Theology*, p. 709.
8. J.I. Packer, *Concise Theology* (Wheaton, IL: Tyndale House Publishers, 1993), p. 162.
9. Wayne Grudem, *Systematic Theology*, p. 970.
10. Robin Boisvert and C.J. Mahaney, *How Can I Change?* (Gaithersburg, MD: People of Destiny International, 1992), p. 32.
11. Anthony Hoekema, *Saved by Grace,* p. 57.
12. Jerry Bridges, *Transforming Grace,* p. 39.

STUDY TWO – No Other Book Like It

1. Octavius Winslow, *The Precious Things of God* (Ligonier, PA: Soli Deo Gloria Publications, reprinted in 1993), p. 250.
2. Millard Erickson, *Christian Theology* (Grand Rapids, MI: Baker Book House, 1985), p. 241.
3. J.C. Ryle, *Matthew*, Vol. 1 of The Crossway Classic Commentaries, Alister McGrath and J.I. Packer, series editors (Wheaton, IL: Crossway Books, 1993), p. 1.
4. Donald Whitney, *Spiritual Disciplines for the Christian Life* (Colorado Springs, CO: NavPress, 1991), p. 33.
5. Ibid., p. 25.
6. Charles Spurgeon, *Morning and Evening: Daily Readings* (Peabody, MA: Hendrickson Publishers, 1991), p. 572.
7. Thomas Brooks, *Precious Remedies Against Satan's Devices* (Carlisle, PA: The Banner of Truth Trust, 1990), pp. 21-22.
8. John Flavel, *The Mystery of Providence* (Carlisle, PA: The Banner of Truth Trust, 1991), p. 13.
9. Donald Whitney, *Spiritual Disciplines for the Christian Life,* pp. 50, 55.
10. R.C. Sproul, *Knowing Scripture* (Downers Grove, IL: InterVarsity Press, 1977)

STUDY THREE – What a Wonderful God You Are!

1. Jess Moody, *A Drink at Joel's Place* (Waco, TX: Word Books, 1967), p. 38.
2. A.W. Pink, *The Attributes of God* (Grand Rapids, MI: Baker Book House, 1975), preface.
3. A.W. Tozer, *The Knowledge of the Holy* (New York: Harper & Row, 1961), p. 9.
4. Thomas Watson, quoted by I.D.E. Thomas in *The Golden Treasury of Puritan Quotations* (Carlisle, PA: The Banner of Truth Trust, 1989), p. 119.
5. Charles Hodge, *Systematic Theology, Volume 1* (Grand Rapids, MI: William B. Eerdmans Publishing Co., 1993), p. 380.

6. Thomas Watson, *A Body of Divinity* (Carlisle, PA: The Banner of Truth Trust, 1992), p. 95.
7. Ibid.
8. Ibid., p. 55.
9. Millard Erickson, *Christian Theology* (Grand Rapids, MI: Baker Book House, 1985), p. 275.
10. Thomas Watson, *A Body of Divinity*, p. 56.
11. J.I. Packer, *Rediscovering Holiness* (Ann Arbor, MI: Servant Publications, 1992), pp. 60-61.
12. A.W. Pink, *The Attributes of God*, p. 28.
13. Charles Hodge, *Systematic Theology, Volume 1*, p. 441.
14. A.W. Pink, *The Attributes of God*, p. 32.
15. A.W.Tozer, *The Knowledge of the Holy*, p. 225.
16. R.C. Sproul, *The Holiness of God* (Wheaton, IL: Tyndale House, 1985), p. 55.
17. Millard Erickson, *Christian Theology*, pp. 284-85.
18. Ibid., p. 285.

STUDY FOUR – The Biggest Decision of Your (New) Life

1. Gordon Fee, *God's Empowering Presence* (Peabody, MA: Hendrickson Publishers, 1994), pp. 5-6.
2. Ibid., p. 6.
3. Ern Baxter, "The Holy Spirit Rediscovered," *People of Destiny* magazine, March/April '89, p. 10.
4. Stanley Horton, *What the Bible Says About the Holy Spirit* (Springfield, MO: Gospel Publishing House, 1976), p. 176.
5. J. Rodman Williams, *The Gift of the Holy Spirit Today* (Plainfield, NJ: Logos International, 1980), p. 15.
6. Bob Sorge, *Exploring Worship* (Canandaigua, NY: Bob Sorge, 1987), pp. 65,66.
7. The phrases *native* tongue, *new* tongue, and *no* tongue are from Arthur Wallis, *Pray in the Spirit* (Fort Washington, PA: Christian Literature Crusade, 1970), p. 90.
8. Ibid., p. 96.
9. Donald Gee, *The Pentecostal Experience: The Writings of Donald Gee*, compiled and edited by David Womack (Springfield, MO: Gospel Publishing House, 1993), p. 35.
10. Stanley Horton, *What the Bible Says About the Holy Spirit*, p. 122.
11. J. Rodman Williams, *Renewal Theology: Salvation, the Holy Spirit, and Christian Living* (Grand Rapids, MI: Zondervan Publishing House, 1990), pp. 199-200.
12. J. Rodman Williams, *The Gift of the Holy Spirit Today*, p. 18.
13. Arthur Wallis, *Living God's Way* (Columbia, MO: Cityhill Publishing, 1988), pp. 39-40.
14. Ibid., p. 41.
15. D. Martyn Lloyd-Jones, *Joy Unspeakable* (Wheaton, IL: Harold Shaw Publishers, 1984), p. 75.
16. Richard Lovelace, *Dynamics of Spiritual Life* (Downers Grove, IL: InterVarsity Press, 1979), p. 131.

STUDY FIVE – Some Things to Know About Yourself

1. David C. Needham, *Birthright* (Portland, OR: Multnomah Press, 1979), p. 47.
2. Jerry Bridges, *The Discipline of Grace* (Colorado Springs, CO: NavPress, 1994), p. 95.
3. Jerry Bridges, *Transforming Grace* (Colorado Springs, CO: NavPress,

1991), p. 39.

4. Quoted by J.I. Packer in *Growing in Christ* (Wheaton, IL: Crossway Books, 1994), p. 80.

5. Thomas a Kempis, *The Imitation of Christ* (Chicago, IL: Moody Press, 1984), p. 30.

6. R.C. Sproul, *TableTalk* (Lake Mary, FL: Ligonier Ministries), June '94, p. 6.

7. Jerry Bridges, *The Pursuit of Holiness* (Colorado Springs, CO: NavPress, 1978), p. 59.

8. John Owen, *The Works of John Owen, Volume VI*, edited by William Goold (Carlisle, PA: The Banner of Truth Trust, 1967), p. 171.

9. Sinclair Ferguson, *John Owen on the Christian Life* (Carlisle, PA: The Banner Of Truth Trust, 1987), p. 140.

10. Ibid., pp. 130-31.

STUDY SIX – Some Things to Know About Your Battle

1. Robert Davis, "Self-Amputee Taking Steps," *USA Today*, 8/31/93.

2. Jerry Bridges, *Transforming Grace* (Colorado Springs, CO: NavPress, 1991), p. 30.

3. Wayne Grudem, *Systematic Theology* (Grand Rapids, MI: Zondervan Publishing House, 1994), p. 490.

4. Quoted by Jerry Bridges in *The Pursuit of Holiness* (Colorado Springs, CO: NavPress, 1978), p. 20.

5. Sinclair Ferguson, *John Owen on the Christian Life* (Carlisle, PA: The Banner of Truth Trust, 1987), p. 132.

6. Ibid.

7. John Owen, *The Works of John Owen, Volume VI*, edited by William Goold (Carlisle, PA: The Banner of Truth Trust, 1967), p. 162.

8. Thomas a Kempis, *The Imitation of Christ* (Chicago: Moody Press, 1980), p. 44.

9. John Owen, quoted in *God's Words* by J.I. Packer (Downers Grove, IL: InterVarsity Press, 1981), p. 185.

10. Sinclair Ferguson, *John Owen on the Christian Life*, p. 146.

11. Richard Sibbes, *The Complete Works of Richard Sibbes*, Vol. 1. (Edinburgh: James Nichol, 1862), p. 200.

12. Lawrence O. Richards, *Expository Dictionary of Bible Words* (Grand Rapids, MI: Zondervan Publishing House, 1985), p. 639.

13. J.C. Ryle, *Holiness* (Welwyn, Hertfordshire, England: Evangelical Press, 1989), p. 68.

14. Tony Sargent, *The Sacred Anointing* (London: Hodder & Stoughton, 1994), p. 142.

15. Obadiah Sedgwick, *The Anatomy of Secret Sins, Presumptuous Sins, Sin in Dominion, and Uprightness* (Morgan, PA: Soli Deo Gloria Publications, 1995), p. 15.

16. Wayne Grudem, *Systematic Theology*, p. 415

17. *The NIV Study Bible* (Grand Rapids, MI: Zondervan Publishing House, 1985), p. 1815.

18. Jerry Bridges, *The Discipline of Grace* (Colorado Springs, CO: NavPress, 1994), p. 46.

19. J.I. Packer, *God's Words*, (Downers Grove, IL: InterVarsity Press, 1981) p. 85.

STUDY SEVEN – Where Do We Go from Here?

1. Randy Alcorn, *Money, Possessions, and Eternity* (Wheaton, IL: Tyndale House Publishers, 1989), p. 140.

2. William Law, *A Serious Call to a Devout and Holy Life* (Grand

Rapids, MI: William B. Eerdmans Publishing Co., 1966), p. 1.

3. Westminster Shorter Catechism, quoted by Thomas Watson in *A Body of Divinity*, (Carlisle, PA: The Banner of Truth Trust, 1992), p. 6.

4. Gary Thomas, "Wise Christians Clip Obituaries," *Christianity Today*, 10/3/94, p. 25.

5. Quoted by Randy Alcorn in *Money, Possessions, and Eternity*, p. 137.

6. Thomas Watson, *A Body of Divinity*, p. 6.

7. Jack Hayford, *The Church On the Way* (Lincoln, VA: Chosen Books, 1982)

8. Robin Boisvert and C.J. Mahaney, *How Can I Change?* (Gaithersburg, MD: People of Destiny International, 1993), p. 81.

9. John Piper, *Desiring God* (Portland, OR: Multnomah Press, 1986), p. 65.

10. Ibid.

11. John R. W. Stott, *The Message of Ephesians* (Downers Grove, IL: InterVarsity Press, 1979), p. 129.

12. J.C. Ryle, *Holiness* (Welwyn, Hertfordshire, England: Evangelical Press, 1989), p. 78.

13. Richard Baxter, *An Alarm to the Unconverted* (Morgan, PA: Soli Deo Gloria Publications, 1990), p. 1024.

OTHER TITLES IN PDI'S *PURSUIT OF GODLINESS* SERIES

DISCIPLINED FOR LIFE   John Loftness and C.J. Mahaney

Are you satisfied with the depth of your devotional life? If you're like most Christians, probably not.

Disciplined For Life puts change within your grasp. Leave the treadmill of spiritual drudgery behind as you discover fresh motivation and renewed passion to practice the spiritual disciplines. (112 pages)

THIS GREAT SALVATION   Robin Boisvert and C.J. Mahaney

Countless Christians struggle through life feeling condemned and confused. No matter how much they do for God, they never feel quite sure of his acceptance.

Sound at all familiar? Then you'll find *great* news in *This Great Salvation*. Start enjoying a new measure of grace and peace at every level of your Christian life as this unique book reveals all God has done for you through Christ. (112 pages)

HOW CAN I CHANGE?   Robin Boisvert and C.J. Mahaney

How Can I Change? (originally titled *From Glory To Glory*) rests on a remarkable assumption: If you will study and apply the doctrine of sanctification, any sin can be overcome.

Have you known the frustration of falling short in your efforts to please God? Have you questioned whether you will *ever* be able to change? If so, this book will have a profound impact on your walk with Christ. (112 pages)

continued on following page...

LOVE THAT LASTS
Gary and Betsy Ricucci

A magnificent marriage is more than wishful thinking. It can and should be the experience of every husband and wife willing to follow God's plan for them as a couple.

Whether your marriage is new, needy, or simply ready for a refresher, here is an excellent guide for helping you build a thriving, lasting love. (176 pages)

WALKING WITH THE WISE
Benny and Sheree Phillips

At last...a book to keep your hopes and standards high during the adolescent years! Written for parents and teens to use together, *Walking With The Wise* hits the "big issues" such as dating, peer pressure, and passion for God.

Reinforce your relationship...and strengthen your convictions...with this one-of-a-kind resource for parents and teens. (192 pages)

WHY SMALL GROUPS?
C.J. Mahaney, General Editor

Not simply a how-to guide, this illuminating book starts by answering the all-important question of *why* a church needs small groups. The short answer? Because small groups are invaluable in helping us to "work out our salvation together" in practical, biblical ways.

Specially developed for leaders and members of small groups alike, *Why Small Groups?* is loaded with insight, wisdom, and practical instruction. This book can put you on the fast track to Christian maturity. (144 pages)

ADDITIONAL RESOURCES FROM PDI COMMUNICATIONS

PRAISE AND WORSHIP MUSIC

PDI worship songs have been in use for more than a decade in local churches around the world. By the grace and mercy of God, more than 10,000 churches in the United States alone currently use these Christ-centered, Cross-centered songs to worship and glorify God. PDI Music's *Come and Worship* series features four releases per year, two of them documenting live worship experiences.

TEACHING TAPES

Powerful messages on growth in holiness, raising teens, the local church, biblical roles for men and women, leadership issues, and much more.

SOVEREIGN GRACE MAGAZINE

In circulation for more than 15 years, this bimonthly publication addresses the most critical issues facing Christians today. It also profiles the people and progress of PDI's team-related churches in the United States and abroad.

For a catalog of PDI resources and a free issue of *Sovereign Grace*, call **1-800-736-2202** or write to us:

PDI Communications
7881 Beechcraft Avenue, Suite B
Gaithersburg, MD 20879

email:pdi@pdinet.org
fax: 301-948-7833
Web site: www.pdinet.org